LOVE AND CAPES

GOING TO THE CHAPEL

STORY AND ART BY:
THOMAS F. ZAHLER

INTRODUCTION

I'm delighted to be here, to introduce the second collection of **Love and Capes** in collected format. From the very first issue, I've enjoyed this series enormously, becau—

It's funny, like a really good situation comedy. I love the little throwaway bits, by Abby and her sister, referencing TV shows I like, or the conversations she has with Mark. I feel like these are people I would enjoy hanging out with.

Uh, yeah. I agree with all that, except I wasn't going to mention TV shows. I like the superhero adventure stuff, of course, because it's clever and dead-on, with an obvious love of what it's spoofing, but I also like Mark and Abby's relationship. The stresses and such that they go through are caused by different things, but the relationship itself is very human, very relatable, and very familiar. Also funny.

My main problem with the series is that I can't keep track of the new issues. I mean that literally. I get a new issue in, and then next thing I know it's disappea—

Well, you don't always tell me what comics have come in. They come in and you squirrel them away into one pile to read, and then another pile after they've been read… by the time I've noticed a new one has come in, it's been stashed somewhere or even filed away and I'll never find it. So I have to grab it as soon as I see it or I don't get to read it until months later.

Tell me about it. I like to sort the comics I'm going to read so the ones I like most are on the bottom, and I get to read better and better stuff as I go through the stack. And then I get to the bottom of the stack and it's not there anymore. And it's not like you put it back once you've read it. You'll just leave it somewhere, and it'll get put into a pile of stuff to be put away, and I'll never see it until the next one comes in and I realize I've missed one. Then I have to scour the house until I turn it up.

But I guess when there's a comic like this, that we both like so much, that's just going to happen. I'm glad we both like it, that there are comics we can share. I'm just fussy about my comics. I like to say where I put them, and when th—

They do stay where you put them, most of them. All over the house, they stay where you put them, unless I pick them up and file them. You could try it once in a while, it'd help you with remembering the alphabet, and lifting all those longboxes is good exercise, and

Okay, okay! It's still good to have a few comics that we share, where we like the same stuff.

Well, you like the superhero stuff, like you said. And your favorite character is…

WITHDRAWN

Abby, probably. And Microdot, but we haven't seen much of her.

And my favorite characters are Charlotte and Darkblade. They're the straightmen for Abby and Mark. Though the girl bonding between Abby and Amazonia was fun to read and the whole wedding day story was poignant.

It was, it was. The whole storyline in this collection is great. I won't spoil it, for anyone who reads introductions before they read the book—hey, that's what they go up front for—but it's not just jokes and romance. It's full of deft plotting, and nifty ideas, and jealousy and exasperation and friendship and character drama… and lots of jokes and romance, too.

I just wish I could get the comic to stay in one place until I've read it. If I try to be good about telling you it's here, can I—

No way. I'm still going to grab the next issue as soon as I see it. It may not be all that long before Sydney's old enough to start reading them and then I'll never see the next issue. It'll disappear into that void she calls a room.

Ack! Good point. Maybe I'd better start reading it first from now on!

Now you're getting somewhere.

[Kurt Busiek is the award-winning writer of **Astro City** and many other fine comic books. Ann Busiek steals his **Love and Capes**. And his **True Story Swear to God** issues, and his **Fables**, and his—

Hey. Who's cooking dinner tonight?

Ann Busiek is a very fine woman with excellent taste in reading material.]

DEDICATED TO LUCILLE AND NORMAN ZAHLER, SR.

YOUR SUNDAY DINNERS WERE—AND STILL ARE—
MY ALGONQUIN ROUND TABLE... BUT WITH BETTER PIE.

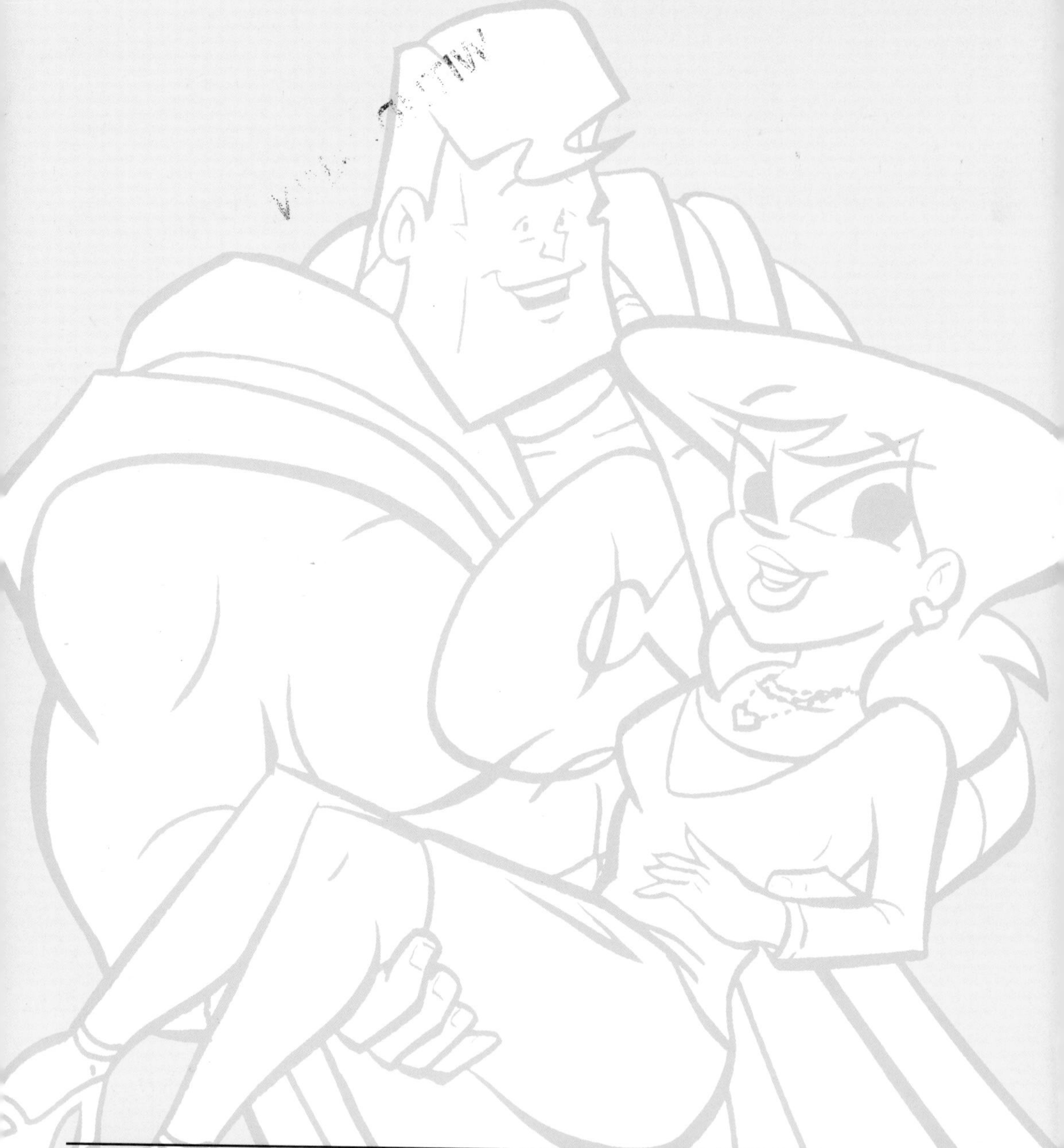

ISBN: 978-1-60010-680-4

15 14 13 12 2 3 4 5

IDW

Ted Adams, CEO & Publisher
Greg Goldstein, President & COO
Robbie Robbins, EVP/Sr. Graphic Artist
Chris Ryall, Chief Creative Officer/Editor-in-Chief
Matthew Ruzicka, CPA, Chief Financial Officer
Alan Payne, VP of Sales

Become our fan on Facebook **facebook.com/idwpublishing**
Follow us on Twitter **@idwpublishing**
Check us out on YouTube **youtube.com/idwpublishing**
www.IDWPUBLISHING.com

Originally published as LOVE AND CAPES Issues #7–12.

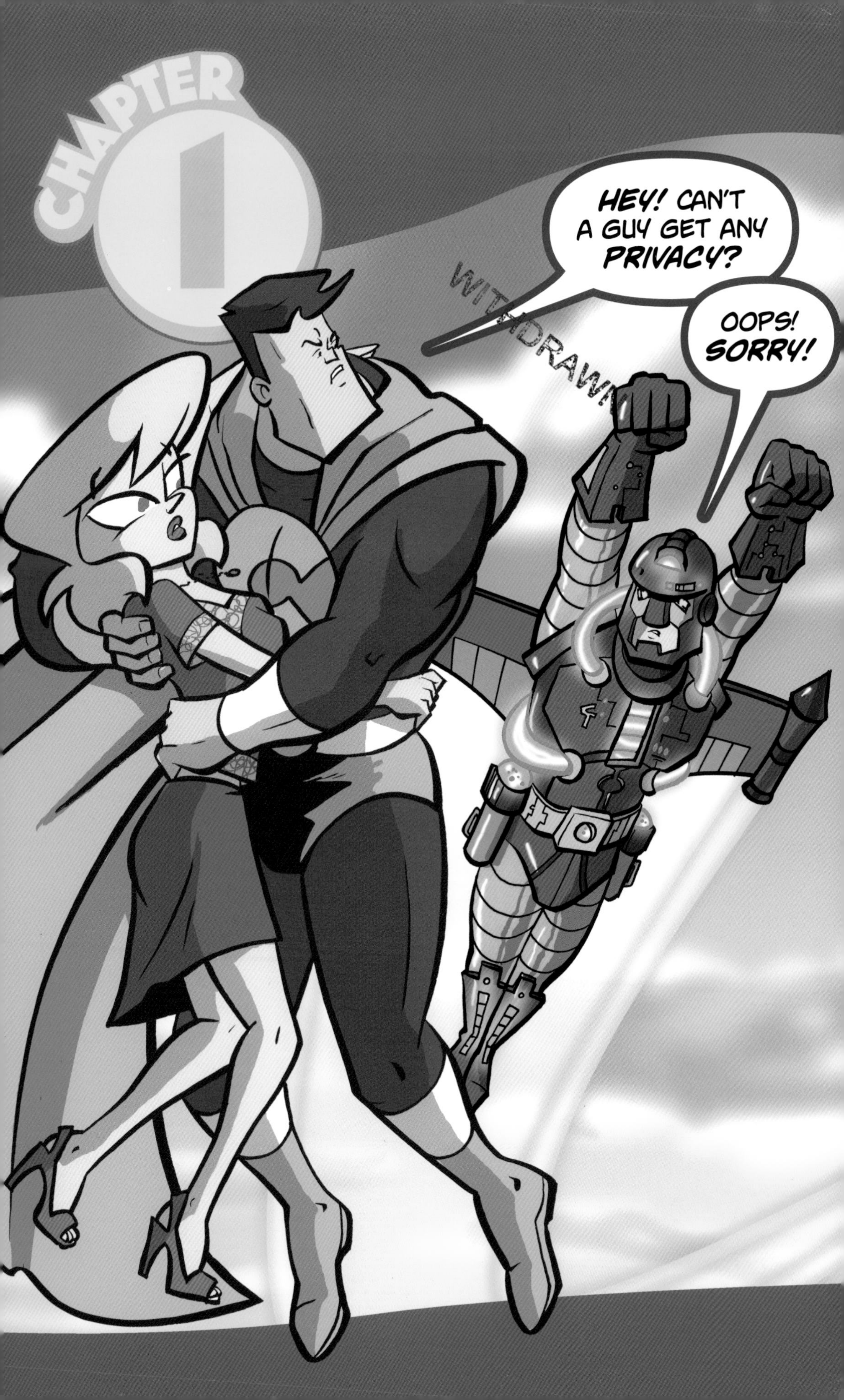
CHAPTER 1
HEY! CAN'T A GUY GET ANY PRIVACY?
OOPS! SORRY!

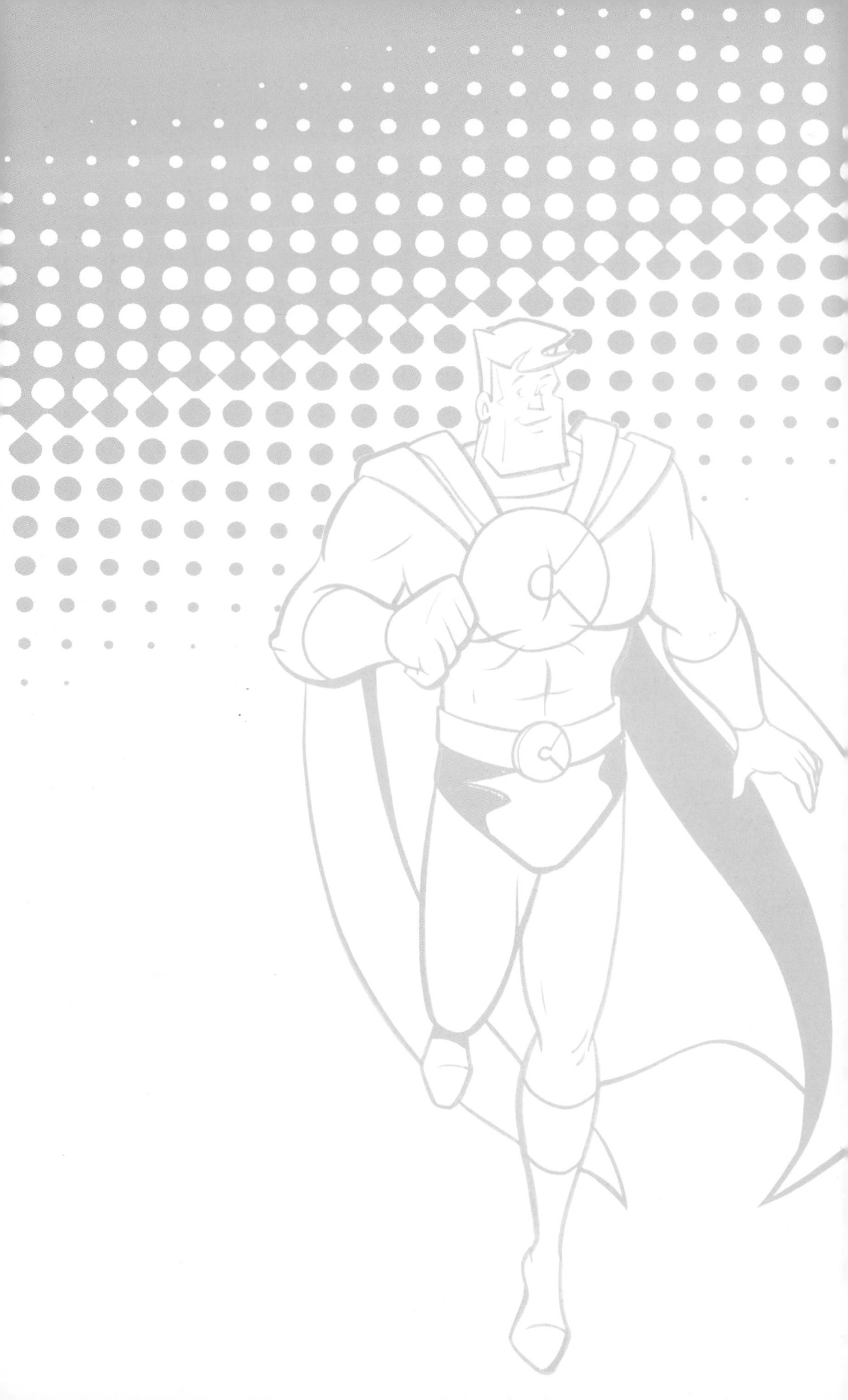

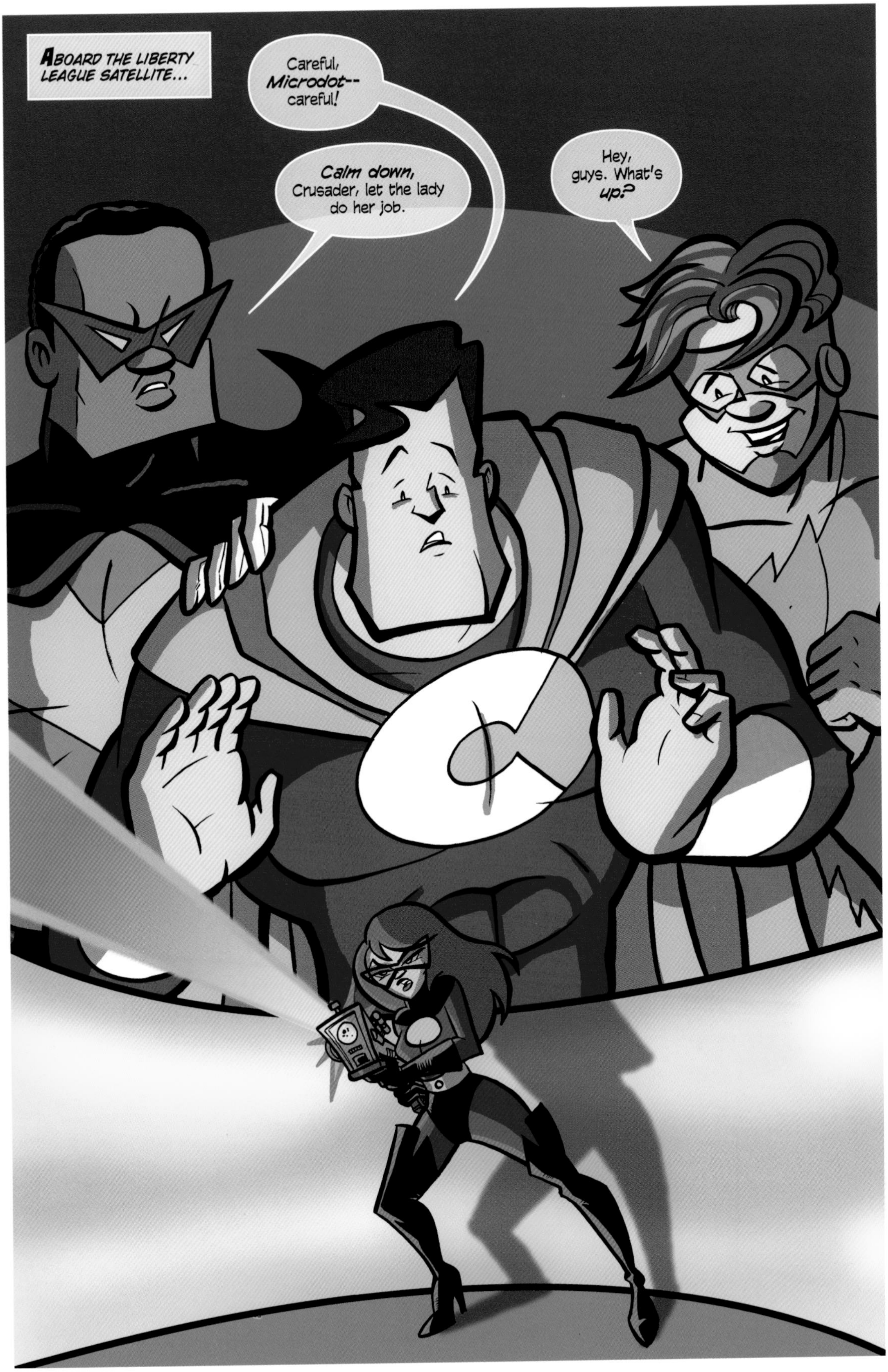
ABOARD THE LIBERTY LEAGUE SATELLITE...
Careful, Microdot-- careful!
Calm down, Crusader, let the lady do her job.
Hey, guys. What's up?

Oh, just doing a little *up-close laser engraving* on the Crusader's *engagement ring.*

Kind of *overkill* if you ask me. But--

--anything for *true love,* right?

And I *appreciate* it, Microdot.

Whoa!

Hey there! I'm Blurstreak.

Yes, your reputation *precedes* you.

Crusader, I have to get *back* to University City--

No problem. Let *me* show you to the *teleporter.*

Gee, thanks.

He works *fast,* doesn't he?

Fastest man on earth.

Looks good. I think *Abby* will like it.

So, *when* are you going to *ask her?*

Christmas Day at her parents' house.

That'll be *some* present.

And, if she doesn't like *this,* I got her the *Jane Austen on Film* DVD set, too.

Always good to have a *backup plan.*

You know, I don't think I've ever seen you this *excited,* Mark.

I love her, Paul. I've *never* been more sure of anything than I am of *this.*

And, watching Blurstreak hit on Microdot makes me realize how *glad* I am I'm out of *that* part of the *dating scene.*

How *does* he get *so many dates* anyway?

Want to get dinner?

Maybe some coffee?

Do you have a MySpace page?

Come on, just give me your number.

⌐Sigh!⌐ All right--

THEN...

So I grabbed a *tuning fork* and--

Oh, yeah! Who's the man? I got her *digits*.

That's funny. She didn't *look* desperate.

Don't be a *hater*. Besides, *you* were quite the *player* back in the day.

Then I *grew up*.

Then you were *kidnapped* by *warrior priests!*

Don't let him get to you, Mike. She seems like a *nice girl*.

Yeah, nice and *hot!*

So when are you going to *call* her?

Not for a couple of days. I've got a date with a *Violet's Closet model* first.

Don't look at me like that. She wanted to *thank me* for saving her from that *fire*. Who am I to say "no"?

I understand *playing the field*, but there's something to be said for *settling down* with the *right* person.

Oh, marriage is a *fine institution*, Mark--

--I'm just *not ready* for an institution.

As far as *settling down*, well--

You see me move *fast*, but for me, the world is in *slow motion*. And I get *bored* being in *one place* for too long.

So you're killing your boredom with a *fast* lifestyle and *fast women?*

Absolutely!

Fast women are the *only* ones who can *keep up* with me.

See ya!

ZOOM!

You see a lot of *yourself* in the Blurstreak, don't you?

A little *too much*, sometimes.

Say, you're going to see *Abby's sister*, too, right?

Yeah. Christmas Day.

Would you mind giving this to *Charlotte*, then? I got her a *little something*.

Sure. No problem.

And *no* taking a *super vision peek!*

Of course not.

Good luck tomorrow. Let me know how it goes.

Hey, um, what did you *wrap this in?*

A new *light refracting cellulose paper* I designed. Good to know it *works*.

CHRISTMAS EVE...

Lock the door, Abby. *Lock the door!*

≀Whew!≀ Another Christmas Eve *survived!*

I would *applaud* us but I'm *too tired*.

Man, if I *never* hear the phrase "She likes those Amazonia Book Club selections a lot..." it'll be *too soon*.

Guess I'd better start *cleaning up*.

Don't worry about it, Charlotte. Let's just *go home*.

Thanks, sis, I--

You can just come in *early* on Tuesday.

Gee, you're *too good* to me.

Kinda wishing you *finished* college now, aren't you?

You know, this will be the *first* year I can remember that you haven't been at *Mom and Dad's* for *Christmas Eve.*

Sharing the holiday is just one of the *perks* of being in a relationship.

Still, I'm *sorry* that you have to suffer a holiday with *Mark's mom.*

Don't be. His Mom's actually been *really nice* this year--

She even called and said she was *looking forward* to seeing me tonight.

Yeah? And *then* what did she say--?

Then she said she made sure she bought *fat-free eggnog* for me.

My work here is *done.*

LATER...

--over at Mom and Dad's.

Hi, honey.

Good evening, ladies. How was the *last shopping day* before Christmas?

Remember when you told us that story about fighting *Duplikid?*

It was like *that,* but instead of being *evil clones,* they were *customers.*

At least charge cards do *less* damage than his *nega-blasters.*

Not to *my* credit rating.

Well, that's *true.*

Have a good *Christmas Eve!* We'll see you tomorrow.

I'm *amazed* you can deal with all those *crowds,* Abby.

Oh, I just focus on the *overflowing* cash register.

It's good to see you haven't lost sight of the *true meaning* of Christmas.

CHARDON, OHIO...

--so *none* of your relatives know you're the *Crusader?*

Nope, just *Mom* and *Dad.*

But you've saved the world what... *two times* this year?

Three. You keep forgetting that *death ray* thing.

Okay, so you've *saved* the world--*and* your relatives--*three times.*

So when they do the normal relative "*what's new*" thing, you tell them--

--about the changes in the *tax code.*

And *you,* of course.

Doesn't it drive you *nuts,* though? Not being able to tell them *anything?*

No. I just think of myself as the *world's greatest Secret Santa.*

THEN...

Merry Christmas you two!

Merry Christmas, Mrs. Spencer.

Merry Christmas, Mom!

How was the "*drive*" in?

Smooth as always.

Abby, would you take the *presents* and *my coat?* I need to talk to my Dad. It's a Christmas thing.

Sure.

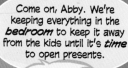

Come on, Abby. We're keeping everything in the *bedroom* to keep it away from the kids until it's *time* to open presents.

Oh, and I'll have to show you the new *commemorative state plate* that I got. Three more and I have the *whole Union.*

That's *great,* Mrs. Spencer.

≳Cough cough!≲

Okay, I know you can hear me, Mark--

--you've got *ten minutes.* I expect to be *rescued* before we hit Wyoming.

Oh, *no,* son. Is there a crisis?

No. Not *yet,* at least.

AND SO...

All right, what did you need to *talk* about, Mark?

Nothing *major*--

--I just wanted to tell you that *tomorrow* I'm going to ask Abby to *marry me*.

Oh, son, that's *fantastic!* She's a *great* woman and you two make a *great couple.*

Thanks, Dad. That means a lot.

Have you told *your mother* yet?

Not *yet*. I was worried that she might not be able to keep the secret *all night.*

She'll be *fine*, Mark.

After all, there's *one secret* she's been keeping for *over ten years* now.

Do you have the *ring* on you?

Please.

I don't let it out of my *sight*. Would you like to *see it?*

Whoa.

Son, that's *some rock*. It must have set you back a *ton*.

No, not really.

You *made* it, didn't you?

Being a superhero means never having to pay *retail*, Dad.

MEANWHILE...

You must be Abby. I'm Mark's cousin, *Hannah*.

Did you just get here, too?

Maybe about *twenty minutes* ago.

Hmmm. That's *funny*. I didn't see your *car* in the drive when we pulled in.

Um, *yeah...* well, that--

Oh, I had Mark park over at the *Thatcher's* so that our drive had *more room*.

Oops, I think that was one of *my* kids. I better check on them.

They're a *handful*, aren't they?

Nice meeting you, Hannah.

Crash!

Don't be *too* hard on yourself, dear. I've just been doing it *longer*.

...

THEN...

Thanks for the *doll*, Uncle Mark!

You should thank *Abby*, too, Elizabeth. She helped me *pick it out*.

Thank you.

Uncle Mark, could you *open it up* for me?

Sure, it's--

Wow. This is *really* in there, isn't it?

What, did they *sew* her hair in there?

Honey, why don't you play with some of your *other* toys. Uncle Mark will bring her over when he's done.

Okay.

Grrr...

Problems?

I've been in *death traps* that were easier to get out of than *this*.

14

AFTER EVERYONE ELSE HAS LEFT...

Did you *tell* your mother--?

Yeah, right after we opened the presents. She seemed *really happy.*

The coast is *clear,* honey.

Thanks for ~sniff~ coming, kids.

Our *pleasure,* Mrs. Spencer.

Yes, it's just--

Are you *okay?*

Come back anytime. You're *always* welcome here. You're *family.*

Come on, Abby. We'd better *go.*

Do you have *any idea* what that big melodramatic goodbye was about?

Oh, Mom *sometimes* gets *overly sentimental* during the holidays.

CHRISTMAS MORNING...

I doubt anyone's *up* yet. They went to midnight Mass last night.

No problem. Superheroes learn to be *very quiet.*

You know, when Charlotte and I were kids, we used to *tackle* anyone who came in with *presents.*

Really?

Yeah, we--

PRESENTS!

You *heard* her coming, didn't you?

Yes, but superheroes also learn that they *can't* save everyone.

They could *try.*

THEN... Bad news, everyone. Quincy's car is *stuck* in a *ditch* and the auto club says they'll take about *two hours* to tow him out.

He's *not* going to be able to make it for Christmas.

Oh, that's *too* bad.

Mark, you're *not* looking well. Do you want to go *upstairs* and lay down for a few minutes?

What? I'm fine, Abby, I--

No. You're looking Quincy... I mean *queasy*.

Trust me, you'll feel better after a nap.

I have a feeling I'll feel a lot *worse* if I *don't* take one.

I'm *sure* that's true.

SHORTLY... Hey, Quincy just called. The auto club must have towed his car *out* while he was inside his house. He'll be here *soon*.

Are you feeling *better*, Mark?

Well, for *now*.

FAR TOO SOON...

Heya, Marky Mark!

Did you see my *sports report* last night?

I'm afraid *not*, Quincy.

Too bad--

It was all about our alma maters being in the *Rose Bowl*.

That's right! You went to *Liberty College*.

Well, *Deco U* is going to *destroy* you guys.

Really? You want to make it *interesting*?

A bet?

Sure, say a *hundred bucks?*

Easy money. You're *on!*

By the way, did you hear that the *entire* Deco U offensive line got *suspended* yesterday in a cheating scandal?

What?

You *really* should watch my sportscast, Mark.

16

THEN...

That was a *Coke*, right Abby?

Yes, please.

You want anything, Charlotte?

Nope. I'm cool.

Hurry up. I want to open *presents!*

Okay, just *breathe*, Spencer. You can do this.

You've faced down both a *Cthulhu demon* and a *plant-eating* giant.

How *hard* can it be--

--to ask *Abby* to *marry* you?

Mark, on *second* thought--

Oh *my*--

Aw, *crap.*

Ohmigod. Ohmigod. *Ohmigod!*

Charlotte, you *have* to be quiet, understand?

I don't want to have to suck *all* the *air* out of the room so you *can't shout.*

Not really. I'm just *making a point.*

Yu kn oo at?

Okay, then.

Mark, this is *fantastic!* I'm *so happy!*

Really?

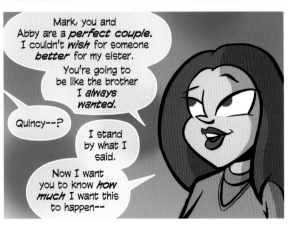

Mark, you and Abby are a *perfect couple.* I couldn't *wish* for someone *better* for my sister.

You're going to be like the brother I *always wanted.*

Quincy--?

I stand by what I said.

Now I want you to know *how much* I want this to happen--

--so that you *believe me* when I tell you that you absolutely, positively *cannot* ask her this way.

What?

Panel 1: What do you mean I *can't* ask Abby to marry me?

You can *ask* her, Mark. Just not *here* or *now*. The ring as Christmas present is a *bad idea*.

Panel 2: But *why?* I know she loves you guys and I thought she'd want to *share* the moment with her family.

Mark, that's sweet. *Wrong*, but sweet.

Panel 3: Women want a proposal to be about her, and *her* alone. Not a *stunt*.

And I know that Abby in *particular* doesn't want to be asked *this way*.

Panel 4: You're *absolutely sure* about this?

She and I have *talked* about this. We're *sisters*, Mark. We share things and *trust* each other.

Man, I could prove this in a *heartbeat* if she hadn't changed where she hides her *diary*.

Panel 5: I *don't know*, Charlotte. I still think--

Wait! I've got it! Give me *fifteen minutes* and I'll prove she *doesn't want* a Christmas proposal.

Panel 6: *PRESENT TIME...*

Why, Quincy, it's a...a *video-tape?*

Yeah! I *finally* found a copy of that Cowboys game that *I played in* that *you* missed.

You mean the one when I was *in the hospital* with appendicitis?

Panel 7: Hey, Abby, I meant to tell you... I ran into Lydia's husband *Tyler* while I was Christmas shopping.

Tyler? Mr. *Christmas Eve Proposal?* I still can't believe she *married him* after that--

Panel 8: *THEN...*

You *okay*, Mark?

Yeah, I'm just *not used* to being the one who gets *saved*.

THEN...

Charlotte, *Paul* asked me to give you this.

We figured we should give it to you on the *QT*.

Unless you've ever figured out a way to tell your parents you know *Paul LaCroix*.

Can't say as I have.

Hmmm, it's a *note*.

I've been awarded the first annual *LaCroix Foundation scholarship* for the arts--

--to the *École du Louvre* in *Paris?*

Whoa.

I'm going outside to get some *air*. Maybe make a *call*.

Did *you* know about this?

If I had, do you think I would have waited to give her *my* present? She won't even *notice* that *Gilmore Girls box set* now.

LATER...

So, *what* are you going to *do*, Char?

I *don't know*, Abby. It *is* a pretty *tempting* offer. And I have been considering *finishing up* my degree.

I *didn't know* you were thinking about *going back* to college.

Well, Paul's been saying I should go *finish up* my *art history degree*.

I've been saying that for a *couple of years* now.

Yes, but *he* says it without that *naggy big sister tone*, so it's much easier to hear. What do *you* think?

Well, as long as you don't try to major in *parties* and *boys* again--

But if they had offered *that* as a major, I probably could have *finished* my degree.

19

THE NEXT EVENING...

--so you didn't ask Abby *at all?*

After almost picking the *exact wrong way* to propose? No.

And now I'm *all paranoid* about doing it right.

I can understand that.

Do *you* have *any* ideas?

Me? I thought the *Christmas proposal* was a good idea. So *no.*

Maybe you can ask *Amazonia.*

What? Ask my *ex-girlfriend* how to propose to my *actual* girlfriend--especially after Zoe wrote that *tell-all?*

Sure, she's got a *female perspective* on this, but... really?

I suppose I could but she *might--wait a minute--*

You're just *messing with me,* aren't you?

What's *surprising* is just how *easy* it is to do.

So what was with the *big gift* to Charlotte. Which, incidentally, would have really *stolen the thunder* from *my* proposal--if I *had* done it.

Ouch! *Sorry* about that.

Well, first, she *deserves* it. She's been thinking about going back, but wasn't sure how to *make it happen.*

Second...you know, we spend so much time helping people by *punching other people* in the face that it's nice to do some good in the world a little *less violently.*

This is *the place,* by the way.

Okay.

Say, you're not *giving up* on punching, are you?

Oh, *heavens no!*

Good to hear.

CRASH!

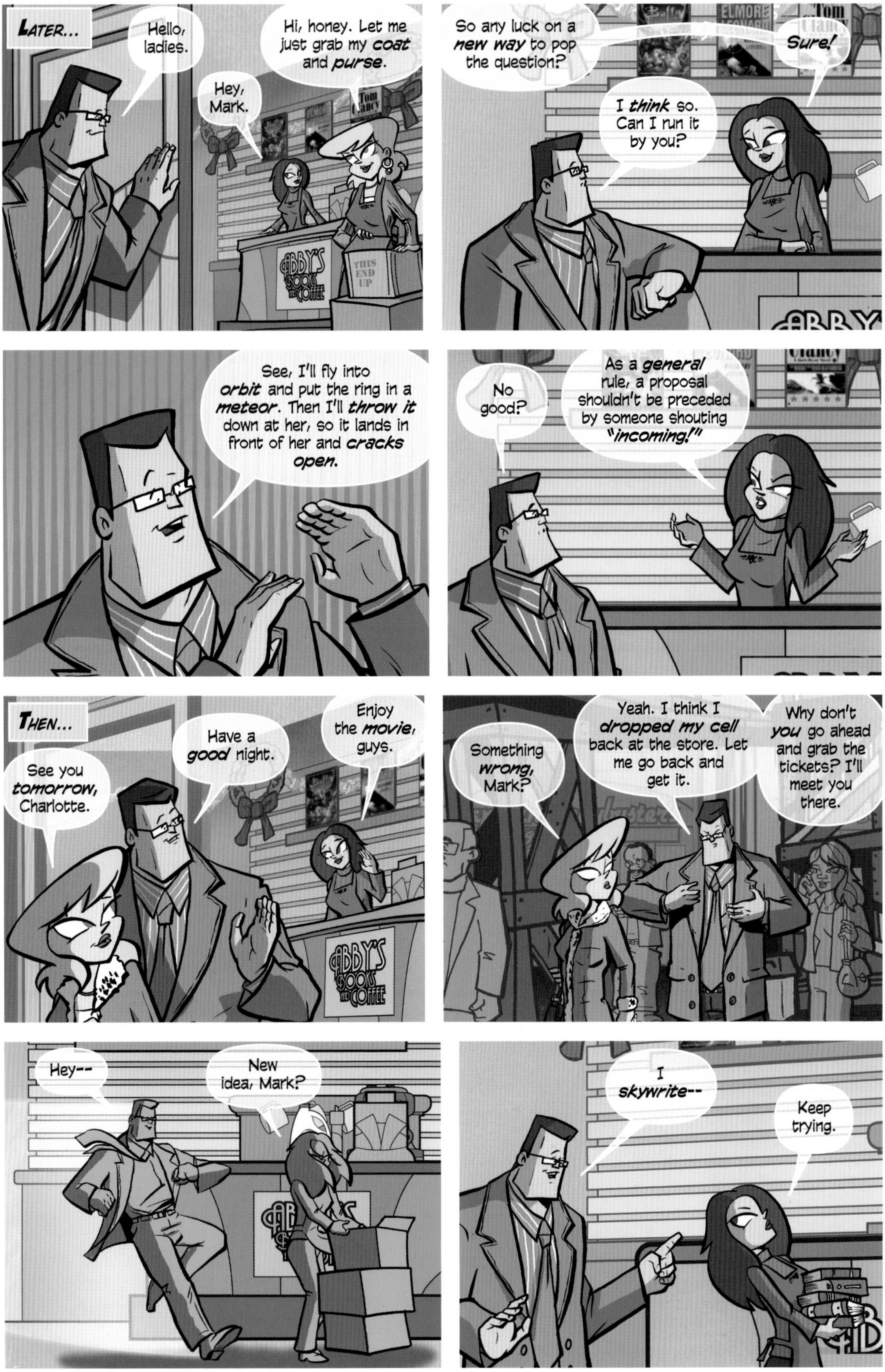
LATER...
Hello, ladies.
Hey, Mark.
Hi, honey. Let me just grab my coat and purse.
So any luck on a new way to pop the question?
Sure!
I think so. Can I run it by you?
See, I'll fly into orbit and put the ring in a meteor. Then I'll throw it down at her, so it lands in front of her and cracks open.
No good?
As a general rule, a proposal shouldn't be preceded by someone shouting "incoming!"
THEN...
See you tomorrow, Charlotte.
Have a good night.
Enjoy the movie, guys.
Something wrong, Mark?
Yeah. I think I dropped my cell back at the store. Let me go back and get it.
Why don't you go ahead and grab the tickets? I'll meet you there.
Hey--
New idea, Mark?
I skywrite--
Keep trying.

THE NEXT DAY...

You don't mind *ordering* it?

Not at all. I'm actually *embarrassed* that we *don't* have it. We--

That's my *cell*. Excuse me.

Mark? *Again?*

‡Groan.‡

Okay, Mark, *hit* me with it... but I warn you, if you're planning on using the words "*stadium*" or "*scoreboard*" just hang up now.

KLIK!

Who was it?

Wrong number.

So *very* wrong.

AND THE NEXT...

Hey, Charlotte. Can I run *another* one by you while I change?

‡Sigh.‡ Mark, look--

I know this is partially my fault, but you're obsessing about this *too much.* Some thought is *good.* Too much is *paralyzing.*

You two love each other. Just *ask* her. Ask her *however* you want. And it'll be *fine.*

Just *be yourself.*

Oh, and make sure there are *flowers.*

There should be *lots* of flowers.

Just be *myself--*

--riiiight.

22

THE NEXT MORNING...

I've *made my decision*, Abby. I *am* going to take Paul up on his scholarship offer.

Good. I was hoping you would.

It's going to be *so exciting!* Living in Paris for a *year*, studying art history at the *Louvre.*

Great food. Great *wine*. Cute Frenchmen with accents.

So I started getting things ready. Yesterday I went to renew my *passport.*

Passport?

Yes, you know-- that thing that allows us *commoners* who actually have to use *airplanes* to travel to other countries.

Hmm. I've always *wondered* how the other half lives.

NOONISH...

I'm getting *hungry*. Are *you* getting hungry?

I'm about ready for lunch. Did you have *any place* in mind?

You know, I have a real *craving* for some tomato soup from *Larry's Soupatorium.*

The *Soupatorium?* But that's halfway *across town* and always has a *huge line.*

Pleeease?

⸮Sigh!⸮ *Fine.* I'll go.

Geez, I *don't* know what you're going to do when I *leave*, though.

I'm probably going to come home to your *dessicated corpse.*

It *just* hit you that I'm leaving for a *year*, didn't it?

I'm going to miss you *so much!*

Miss your *sister* or your *wage slave* lunch getter?

Can't it be *both?*

23

THE NEXT DAY...

I *thought* you might like it.

Well this is *nice*.

What prompted *this?*

Well, the last couple weeks have been pretty *hectic* with the holidays and all--

--and I wanted to see if we could get some time *away* from it all--

Crusader! You mind giving me a *hand?*

--but I guess that's *too much* to ask for.

Oops! Sorry.

THEN...

Are you *sure* you can handle them *alone*, Steel Worker?

Yeah! It's just the *Hardware Twins.* They're pretty low maintenance.

So, *where* were we?

I was *about* to tell you that there was another rea--

BOOM!

They've *upgraded...*

Yeah, um, I'm going to need to *take this.*

I kind of *figured.*

Later...

Thanks for hanging out, Abby. Monitor duty can get pretty *boring*.

Glad to do it, Mark.

It's pretty quiet, maybe later we can go to the *observation deck* and--

Hi, guys!

Why does God *hate* me?

Hello, Blurstreak. What brings *you* up here?

I needed the workout room to *practice* for the annual *charity race* between me and Crusader here.

Oh, yeah. I'd *forgot-ten* that was coming up.

Yeah, you *almost* beat me last year.

I *would have*, too, if you hadn't *cheated* and *vibrated* through that train!

The only rule was "*speed powers only*."

Don't *hate* the player, hate the *game*.

Then...

So, Abby, *tell me* about how Mark p--

--ro--

ZOOM

Mike, I *haven't* asked her yet!

Whoa! Sorry, dude, I *didn't know*.

ZOOM

What was *that* all about?

Oh, just a *running joke*.

By the way, I'm *definitely* faster.

CHRONOPOLIS...

--so Blurstreak almost *blew* the whole thing?

It's *my* fault, really. You'd think after years of keeping the *big secret*, I'd know how to keep the *smaller ones*.

Still, he *should* have noticed Abby *wasn't* wearing the ring.

I need to talk to him about actually *looking* at things.

Not *every-one* can be all Sherlock Holmes like you, Paul.

It's really nothing more than *simple observation*.

Right. Like those *three gunman* I'm observing hiding in that *van* by the *bank?*

Not everyone can observe *through solid objects*, either Mark.

To-*may*-to, to-*mah*-to.

SHORTLY...

So you're going to ask her *tonight?*

Yup. At sunset.

How are you--

Nope, *not* gonna say.

Charlotte saved me from a *big mistake*, but after that, the whole thing just got *inside my head* and I kept overthinking it.

So I'm going *simple*, but I'm also keeping it to *myself*. I don't want any opinions *coloring* my view, you know?

Don't worry, I *get* it. And I'm sure it'll go *just fine*. Good luck.

Thanks, but I *won't* need it. This one's *too simple* to screw up.

Now if you'll *excuse me*, it's almost *sunset* in Deco City.

MEANWHILE...

Hey, honey, it's *me*. I know we were supposed to *go out* tonight, but I'm going to be *stuck at work*--

26

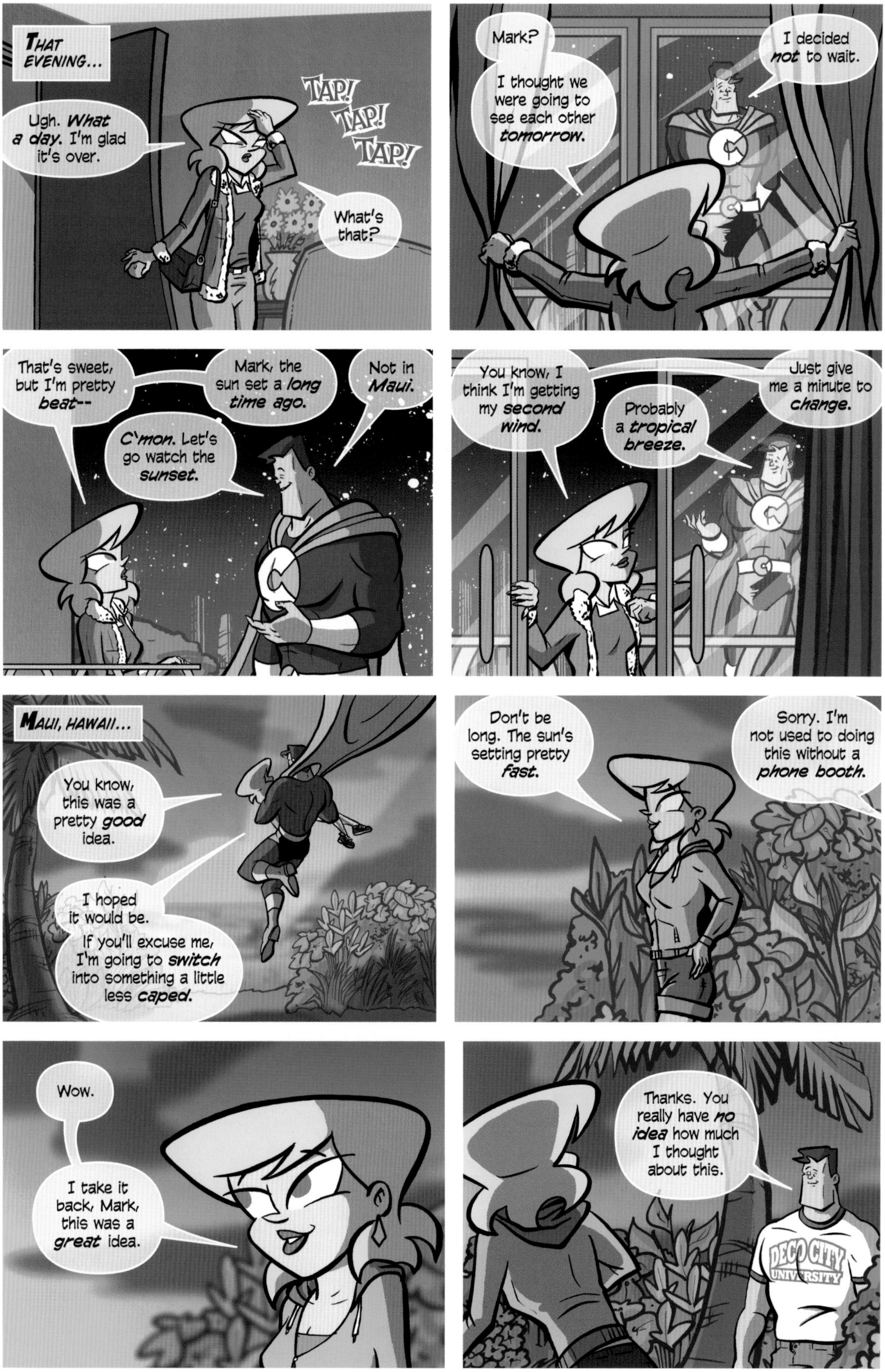
THAT EVENING...
Ugh. What a day. I'm glad it's over.
TAP! TAP! TAP!
What's that?
Mark?
I thought we were going to see each other tomorrow.
I decided not to wait.
That's sweet, but I'm pretty beat--
Mark, the sun set a long time ago.
Not in Maui.
C'mon. Let's go watch the sunset.
You know, I think I'm getting my second wind.
Probably a tropical breeze.
Just give me a minute to change.
MAUI, HAWAII...
You know, this was a pretty good idea.
I hoped it would be.
If you'll excuse me, I'm going to switch into something a little less caped.
Don't be long. The sun's setting pretty fast.
Sorry. I'm not used to doing this without a phone booth.
Wow.
I take it back, Mark, this was a great idea.
Thanks. You really have no idea how much I thought about this.
DECO CITY UNIVERSITY

What's *that* look for?

I just haven't *seen* you like that in a while. Like--

--like *myself?*

It's kind of *weird*, isn't it? I'm usually *Mark Spencer*, accountant, or the *Crusader*.

I *rarely* get to be just *me*. And you're probably the *only* person on the planet who gets to see me like this. Like *me*.

But *this* is how I see myself. *This* is the person who I see when I look in the mirror in the morning.

And it's *important to me* that you get to see this person.

Because *this*--

--this is the *person* asking you to be his *wife*.

So, Abigail Tennyson--

--will you *marry me?*

C'mon, it doesn't even have to be a *whole sentence*. Just something? *Anything?*

Just *one* word...?

28

YES!

Yes, yes, *yes!*

Abby, I don't have the words to describe *how happy* you've just made me.

The feeling is *more* than *mutual.*

I *can't stop* smiling. It's just--

--it's *intoxicatingly* good.

I know what you mean. I'm *walking on air* myself.

LATER...

⸮Sigh!⸮

I'm glad I decided to propose *this* way.

You had *another* way in mind?

Yeah. I *was* going to ask you Christmas Day at your parents' house.

Really?

Oh, Lord, that would have been *horrible.* I hate Christmas proposals with a *fiery passion.*

It's a *good thing* you didn't do that.

Oh?

Don't worry, I still would have said *"yes."*

I just *wouldn't* have been *happy* about it.

29

So *what* stopped you from asking me on Christmas?

Charlotte.

She found out I was going to propose and steered me *away* from *that* one.

I'll have to *thank her* when we get back.

I tried to ask you a couple more times after that, but it *never worked out.*

So I was going to ask you tonight back in *Deco City*, but *you* had to work late.

Ouch. *Sorry* about that.

And then I remembered something *else* Charlotte said--

"Make sure there are *plenty* of *flowers*."

Well, you did *good*, my super fiancé.

I do have a *favor* to ask, though.

Engaged for *twenty minutes* and you're *already* being demanding.

What is it?

I get to tell Amazonia!

END

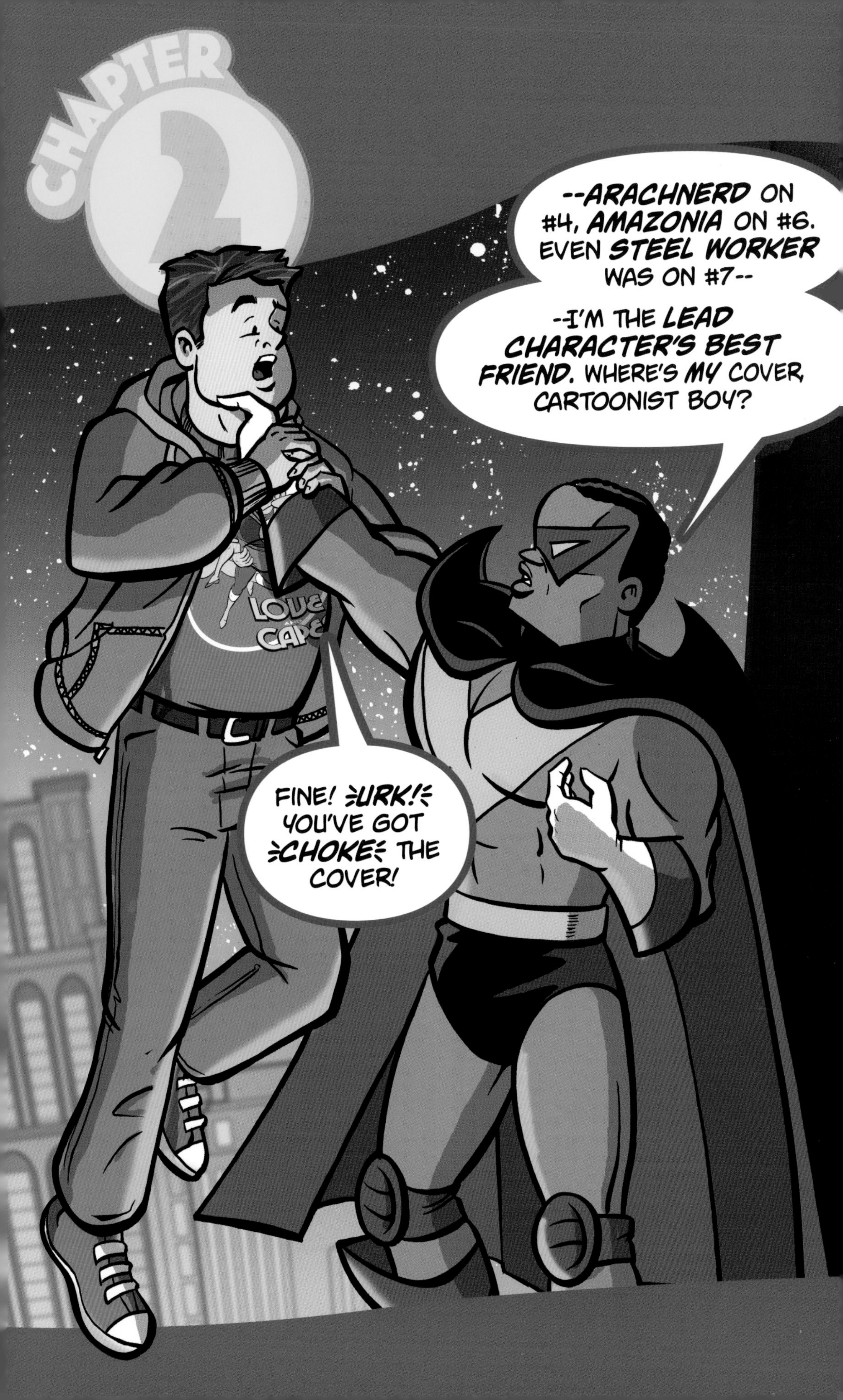
CHAPTER 2
--ARACHNERD ON #4, AMAZONIA ON #6. EVEN STEEL WORKER WAS ON #7--
-I'M THE LEAD CHARACTER'S BEST FRIEND. WHERE'S MY COVER, CARTOONIST BOY?
LOVE AND CAPES
FINE! URK! YOU'VE GOT CHOKE THE COVER!

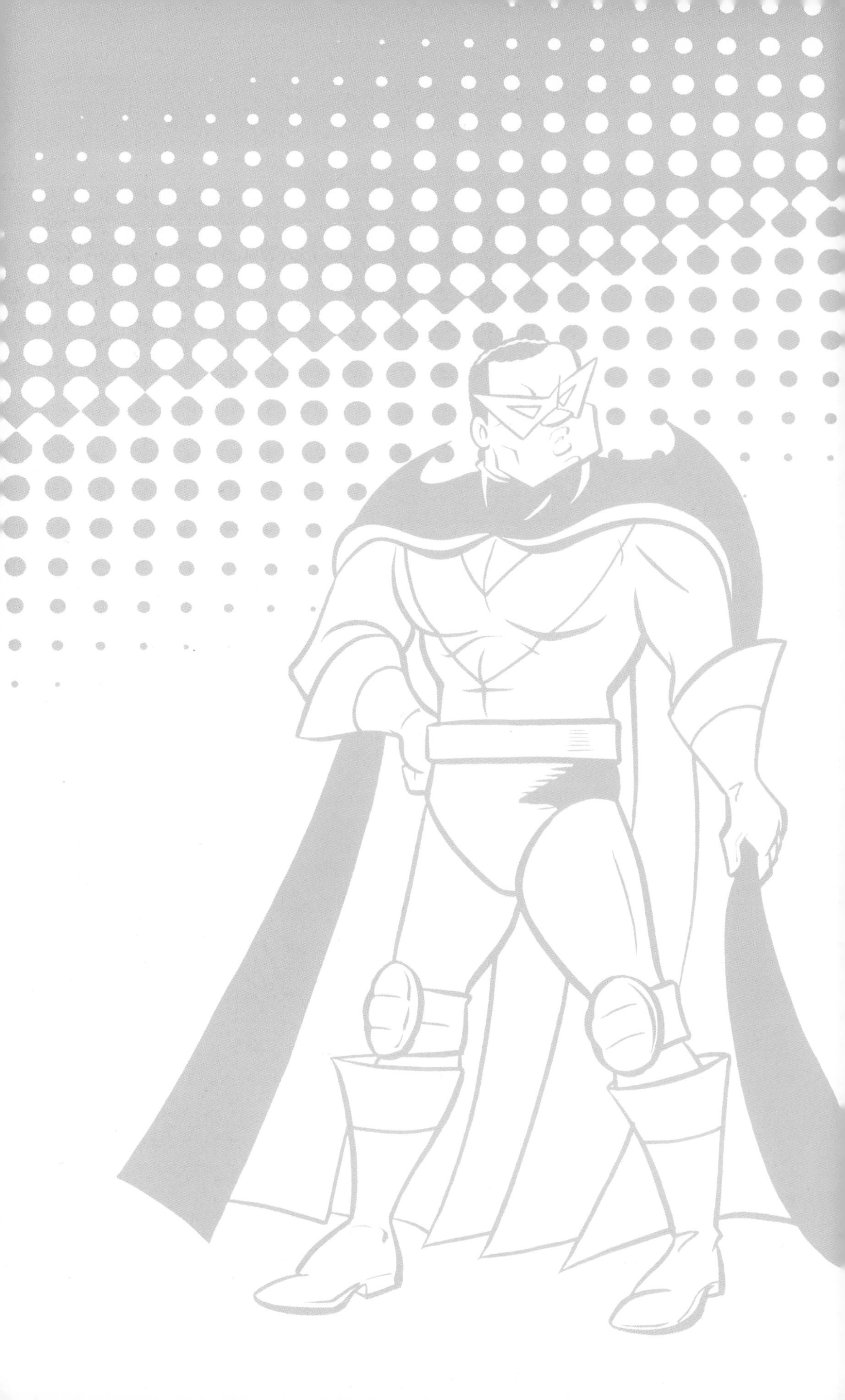

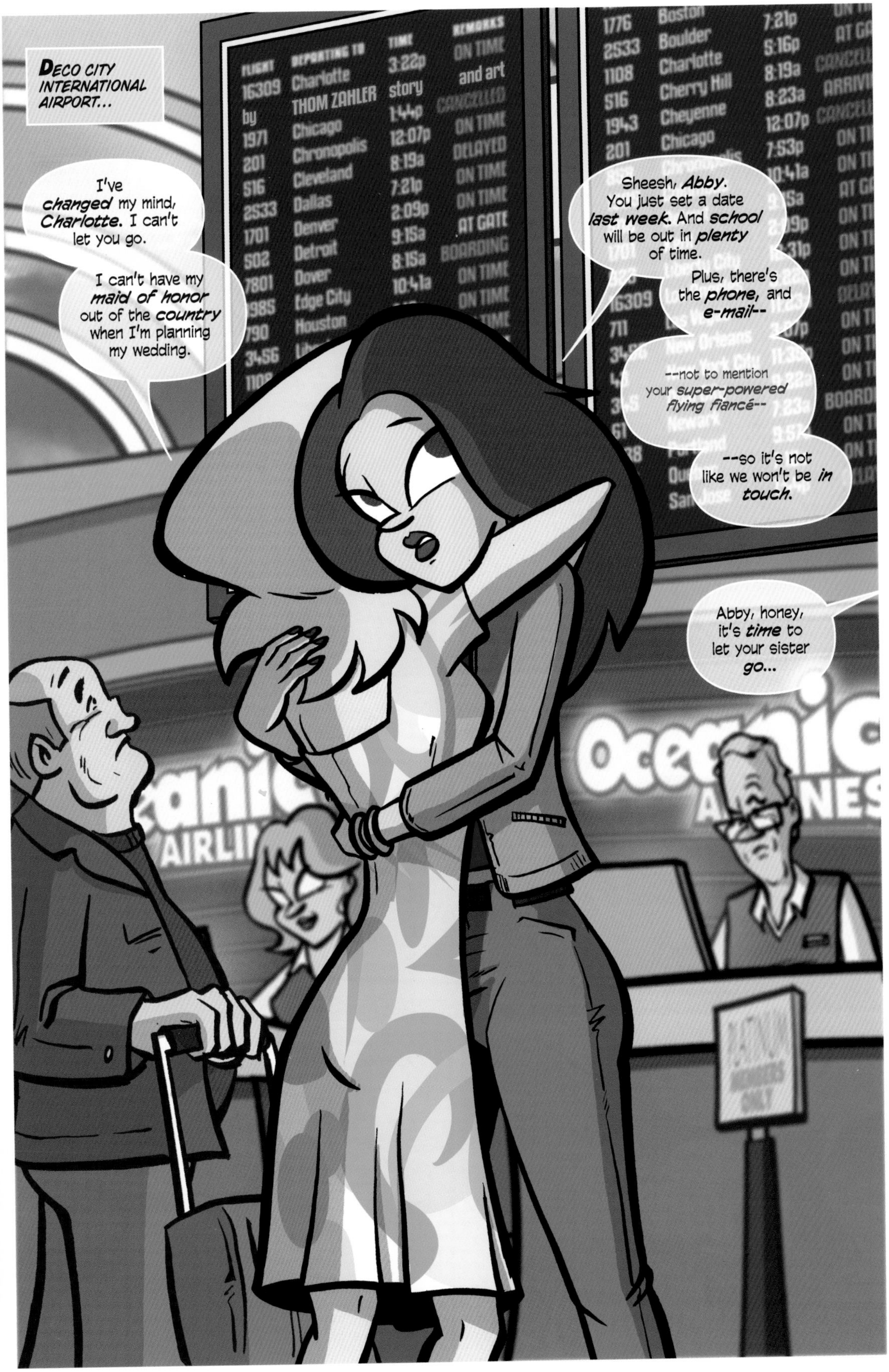
DECO CITY INTERNATIONAL AIRPORT...
I've changed my mind, Charlotte. I can't let you go.
I can't have my maid of honor out of the country when I'm planning my wedding.
Sheesh, Abby. You just set a date last week. And school will be out in plenty of time.
Plus, there's the phone, and e-mail--
--not to mention your super-powered flying fiancé--
--so it's not like we won't be in touch.
Abby, honey, it's time to let your sister go...

...Charlotte has a *plane* to catch.

⊰Sniff.⊱ *Okay.*

How *long* is your flight again, dear?

Fifteen hours, counting my layover in *Chronopolis.*

Let me make sure I--*crap!* I forgot I had this *water bottle* in here. Will you take it, Mom?

You're *not allowed* to take water on the plane anymore?

Nothing over *three ounces.* It's a *security thing.*

Just the *TSA* keeping our *skies safe.*

⊰Cough! Cough!⊱

Of course, I'm sure they're not the *only* people keeping them safe.

Probably not.

Okay, Future Sister-In-Law, you have a *good time* in *Paris.*

And if you need *anything--*

--I'll be sure to *call,* Future Brother-In-Law. And *you* keep an eye on Abby. She will *definitely* be stressing out over the wedding.

First suggestion: *hide the caffeine.*

Good-bye, honey.

Dad--Mom-- I'm going to miss you guys *sooo* much.

We'll miss *you,* too, dear.

Tell *Quincy* I'm sorry he couldn't make it.

Bye, everyone! *École du Louvre here I come!*

Call us when you get there.

You've got your *passport,* right?

Remember you're allergic to--

Abby--

--stop *ruining* the moment.

Sorry.

SHORTLY...

Charlotte will be *fine*, Abby.

I *know*, Mom. I'm just going to *miss* her.

We *all* will, dear. I'm *glad* she's getting to study abroad and finish her degree, but it'll be odd not having her at the *house*.

Well, *I'll* be stopping by a *lot* more. I'll need *someone* to help me with the wedding plans.

I'm *surprised* how much there is to do.

You know what surprises *me?* Charlotte managing to bring only *one* bag. I was sure she'd have at least three.

Well, some people will do *anything* to avoid those *extra bag charges*.

YESTERDAY...

What are *you* looking at?

Nothin'.

THEN...

I've got some *tax stuff* and a *League meeting* so I might not be over tonight.

Don't worry about it. I've got *interviews* to fill Charlotte's position most of the day anyway.

Then I'll see you *tomorrow*. Love you.

Love *you*, too.

You should wear *dresses* more often, by the way.

Thanks, I--*wait a minute...*

Not funny, Spencer!

Sorry, kinda *is*.

35

THEN... So, *Ashley,* you live just a couple of blocks from here?

ABBY'S BOOKS AND COFFEE

Help Wanted

Yeah, my apartment's over on *Fillmore.*

And why did you *leave* Atomic Coffee?

Well, I really didn't like *handling all the money.* Math's just *not* my thing, y'know?

Um, you *know* you'd have to handle money *here,* right?

Really? I thought people just came here to, like, *borrow* books.

Like a *library?*

You mean this *isn't* a library?

Haven't *been* to many, *have* you honey?

ABBY'S INTERVIEWS CONTINUE...

Embezzling, eh?

Really? Do you have-- --y'know... *no.* I'm still going to pass.

Well, the *indictment did* say I was one of the *top* financial experts in the field.

LATER...

--do you have to be a *reader* to work here?

It'd be *nice* if you read, but you don't have to be a *bibliophil--* --oh, Lord, you mean being *able* to *read,* don't you?

AND... No, hangovers are *not* an acceptable excuse for missing work.

FINALLY... Maybe a *helper monkey--?*

Or a *robot.* Mark's got to know someone who can make a *robot.*

AFTER THE LIBERTY LEAGUE MEETING...

I notice that *Amazonia* didn't show again.

That's the *second* time now, isn't it?

Does she think you're *still* mad at her for writing that *tell-all?*

I don't know.

Are you still mad?

What do *you* think?

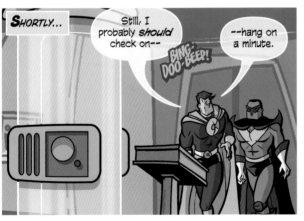

I think that people who think you can't do *dark and broody* don't give you enough credit.

In fairness, I usually *am* standing next to *you.*

SHORTLY...

Still, I probably *should* check on--

--hang on a minute.

BING-DOO-BEEP!

Hi, honey.

Hmm? Yeah, I *suppose* I can do that on the way home.

Love *you,* too.

And so it *begins.*

Don't you *start* with me, Paul.

So what do you have to do? Pick up some *milk* and *bread* on the way *home?*

You're just *jealous.*

That's a *good* one. I'll tell that to the *Maxim cover model* I'm having dinner with tonight.

SOMEWHERE OVER THE ATLANTIC...

What the--

ABBY WANTED ME TO CHECK IN ON YOU!!

SLAM!

Headache?

Sister.

THEN...

Okay, your *sister* is just fi--

Abby, what's *wrong?*

Between wading in the *shallow end* of the *workforce pool* and actual *customers*, I didn't have time to do *anything* else.

So I've still got to *unbox and display* all these books for to--

-mor-

WHOOOSH!

-row.

I crushed the *boxes* and put them in the recycling bin, too. I hope that's okay.

You are *so* hired.

You know, I actually *could work here* for a bit.

It's not the *busy season* for taxes, and with my *speed* and all, I could probably swing it.

At least until you find the *right person* to replace Charlotte.

Oh, Mark, you really are *my hero!*

Keep in mind, though, that I might need to *rush out* every once in a while to *save the world*.

As long as you remember to *clock out* first.

Say, you don't have any *corporate rules* about co-workers not being able to *date*, do you?

Don't worry. In *your* case, Abby's *Books and Coffee* has a *pro-*sexual harassment policy.

39

Paris...

Hey, Abby, it's Charlotte.

You know it's *one in the morning* here, right?

Yeah, but I figured you *wouldn't* be able to sleep until you *knew* I was in okay.

Deco City...

Tragically, you're *quite* mistaken.

Sorry. Well, you're up *now.*

Barely.

Did you manage to find a *replacement* for me today?

Not quite. Mark's going to fill in until I can find someone.

You know, that's the *nicest* thing you've ever said to me.

Don't confuse my *sleep-addled brain.* What do you mean?

Think about it.

The *only* person who could replace me is a *super hero.*

⌐Sigh.⌐

Good night, Charlotte.

The next morning...

Half an hour late, Mark?

Yeah, sorry, I--

You'd *better* have a *good* excuse.

I dunno--

--is stopping *Power Glove* from destroying the *moon* a good one?

Well, it better not happen *again.*

Unless he can figure a way to get his glove out of the *earth's core,* I think we're *good.*

THE NEXT DAY...

You *have* it?

"Couplehood?" Of *course* we have it. It's in the Humor section.

THIS END UP

≥Sigh!≤

Mark, what's *wrong?* You're *glooming up* the store.

Oh, it's just that at *normal* speed this is pretty bo--

--bo--

--bodacious?

Still *too slow*, Hero Boy.

THE DAY AFTER...

Now, you know what *I* went through, Mark.

Has she made you pick up *lunch* yet? She used to send me all the way *across town.*

Yeah, same thing. Except she sent me across the *country.*

She had a taste for *In-and-Out Burg--*

--I have to let you *go*, Charlotte. Talk to you soon.

Whoa, Mark! *Watch it!*

Sorry.

Hey, *guys*, wait up!

Ow! Dude!

You know, I *was* kind of hoping *this* job would be a break from my *other* one.

So there are a lot of *shoplifters* in the *accounting* business?

AFTER A WEEK OF WORKING TOGETHER...

Wha--sorry, honey, Darkblade has an *emergency*. I have to go.

Oh, thank God.

CHRONOPOLIS...

Wait, so you *lied* to Abby and said there was an emergency just so you could *leave?*

I know, I know. I guess it's just been *too much* together-ness

Correct me if I'm wrong, but isn't that the *whole point* of that marriage thing you proposed?

Paul, I want to come home *to her* every night--

--I just don't want to come home *with* her every night.

The *worst* part is, I can tell she feels the *same* way.

So *what* are you going to do?

There's not much I *can* do, except hope she hires someone *soon.*

Well, just in case she asks, *what* was the *emergency* that I called you for?

I dunno-- isn't it *Crisis season?*

THE NEXT DAY...

Thanks for letting me come in *early*, Ms. Tennyson. I've got a 9:30 class.

It's no problem, Jason. What are you studying?

I'm in *film school*, Ms. Tennyson.

Okay, if *I* do hire you, the *first* thing you're going to have to do is learn to call me *Abby*.

You *were* working at Triangle Video. *Why* did you leave there?

A video store is a *dangerous place* for a film student to work, Ms. Te-- Abby.

I didn't *save* much money, but I did amass a pretty *awesome DVD collection.*

I can *definitely* relate.

You do?

Are you *kidding?* I started *this* place so I could *write off* my *book buying habit.*

So let me tell you about the *job.*

Obviously there's *sales* and *ringing register.*

We also try to stock a good mix of *rare* and *mass market* books.

Right now my fiancé has been *kind enough* to fill in--

Oh... hi.

--and *apparently* he came in *early.*

That was your *fiancé?*

Um, yeah.

What was he doing with that *empty box?*

Empty?

Welcome to *Abby's Books and Coffee*, Jason.

Sorry about that, Abby. I didn't realize you had an **interview**.

So, other than **oblivious**, how is he?

It's **my** fault. I forgot to tell you it got **moved up**. Don't worry, though, he **didn't** notice anything.

I think we have a **winner**. He's starting tomorrow.

So I'm--

--**fired**.

It's for the best anyway, Mark. I love you **dearly** but **working** with you, too--it was just **too much**.

It was so amazingly **sweet** of you to help me out. But I'm **not sure** our future marriage would have **survived** much more.

Don't worry. I agree **completely**.

At least I earned a little **extra money**.

Oh, honey... you thought I was **paying** you?

Okay, we **clearly** need to work on our communication skills.

THE NEXT NIGHT...

Oh, Jason worked out **fine**, Mark. He's going to be **great**.

⸘Groan!⸘

Unfortunately, we had a crazy rush right **after** he left.

So he seems to be good for **business**, too.

You know, today's the first day in over a **week** I haven't seen you **at all**.

Yeah. Is it okay if I say it's been kind of **nice**?

Sure--

--I'll just take my bottle of **ice wine** and **go home**.

Well, let's not go **overboard** with this "personal space" thing.

Maybe just **baby steps** instead of doing it all in a **single bound**?

44

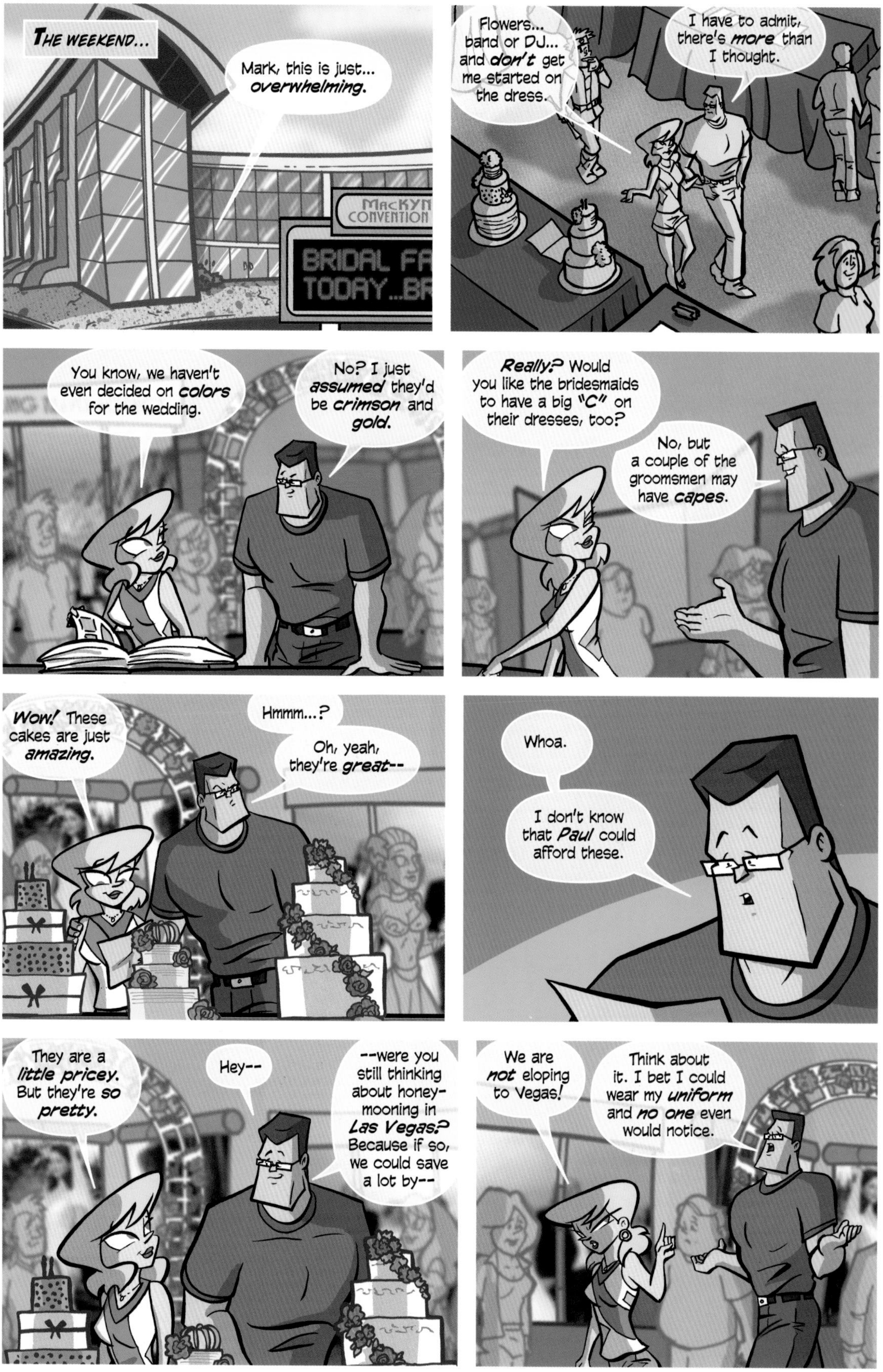
THE WEEKEND...
Mark, this is just... *overwhelming.*
MACKYN CONVENTION
BRIDAL FA
TODAY...BR
Flowers... band or DJ... and *don't* get me started on the dress.
I have to admit, there's *more* than I thought.
You know, we haven't even decided on *colors* for the wedding.
No? I just *assumed* they'd be *crimson* and *gold.*
Really? Would you like the bridesmaids to have a big "*C*" on their dresses, too?
No, but a couple of the groomsmen may have *capes.*
Wow! These cakes are just *amazing.*
Hmmm...?
Oh, yeah, they're *great--*
Whoa.
I don't know that *Paul* could afford these.
They are a *little pricey.* But they're *so pretty.*
Hey--
--were you still thinking about honey-mooning in *Las Vegas?* Because if so, we could save a lot by--
We are *not* eloping to Vegas!
Think about it. I bet I could wear my *uniform* and *no one* even would notice.

Mark, have you noticed anything *strange* here?

Um, like what?

Like the girl in the *Princess Leia Slave Girl outfit?*

No, I must have--

Deco City Comic-Con
HALL B

Aw, crap.

There's a comic book convention here, too?

Wait! *Where* are we going?

Why?

Come on, I *gotta* see this.

With *you* as my fiancé? Are you *kidding?*

I'm *not* going to win this one, am I?

Nope. But *buck up*, how bad can it be?

You mean now that you've *jinxed* us?

TWO ADULT ADMISSIONS LATER...

Hey, look! They've got *Crusader* comics on sale. I didn't know they made those.

Yeah, *Paul* arranged the *license* last year.

And the *quarter bin* isn't a sale, it's an *insult.*

Wow! A *Crusader action figure!* You know, if we pair this with a *Barbie*, we could put them on the *wedding cake.*

Abby, put that *down.*

Geez, couldn't you have at least found the *Diamond Select* figure?

Well, I--

Oh, my--

Salutations, fellow comic fans!

Sweet Lord, it's like that image *burned* into my *brain.*

Really? "*How bad could it be?*"

So was that *unfortunately dressed fan* the reason you dislike these conventions so much?

No. Although it certainly *doesn't* help.

I'm a *comic book fan.* I *get* the whole con thing.

But when I became...*you know*...it stopped being just an *escape.*

Their fantasy is *my reality.*

I guess I'm kind of like a *doctor* who doesn't like watching *"ER"* or *"Grey's Anatomy."*

Plus, there's just a *lot* of--

Holy--!

It's a *DVD* of *"The Crusader on Ice!"*

--lousy merchandise.

Yup, someone with a camcorder shot the *whole "Crusader on Ice"* production.

That is *so cool!*

That is *so illegal.*

In fact, just to *defend copyright,* I'm going to use my *magnetic resonance vision* --

--to *erase* that DVD.

You *really* think I don't know that DVDs are *optical* and *not magnetic?*

Razzle... frazzle...

I'll take this. You really have *no idea* how much I've wanted to see it.

I mean *really.*

47

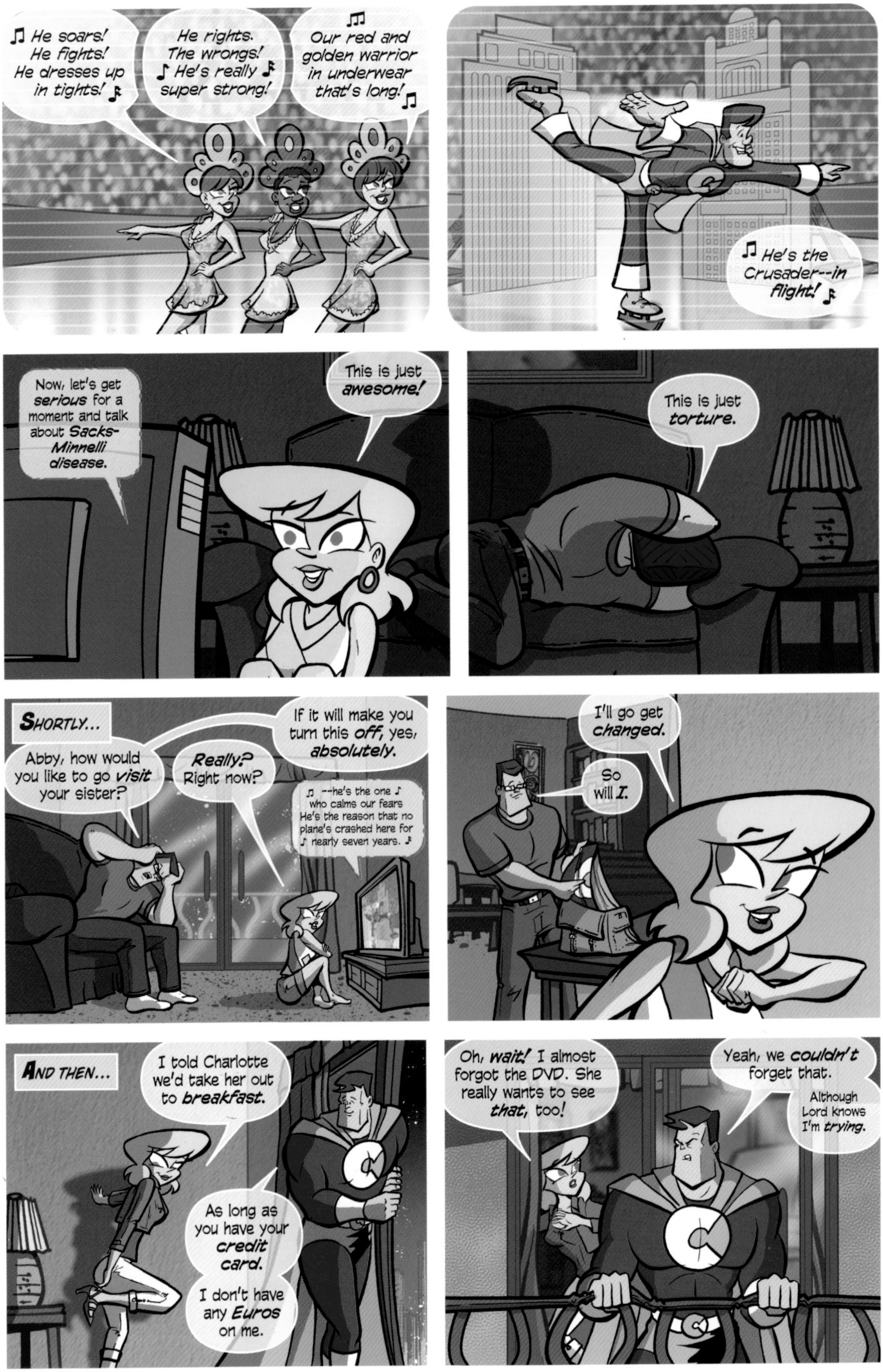
♫ He soars! He fights! He dresses up in tights! ♪
He rights. The wrongs! ♪ He's really ♪ super strong!
♫ Our red and golden warrior in underwear that's long! ♫
♫ He's the Crusader--in flight! ♪
Now, let's get serious for a moment and talk about Sacks-Minnelli disease.
This is just awesome!
This is just torture.
SHORTLY...
Abby, how would you like to go visit your sister?
Really? Right now?
If it will make you turn this off, yes, absolutely.
♫ --he's the one ♪ who calms our fears He's the reason that no plane's crashed here for ♪ nearly seven years. ♪
I'll go get changed.
So will I.
AND THEN...
I told Charlotte we'd take her out to breakfast.
As long as you have your credit card.
I don't have any Euros on me.
Oh, wait! I almost forgot the DVD. She really wants to see that, too!
Yeah, we couldn't forget that.
Although Lord knows I'm trying.

PARIS...

I *think* that's her, Mark. But I'm *not sure*, it's been *so long*.

Or *maybe* it's just that you're much *older* than me and your *memory* is *going*. Still--

--I have to say, I've missed you *more* than I *thought* I would.

I told you so.

Okay, I didn't so much miss *that*.

Abby, I think something's *wrong*.

Mark?

What the *frak*?

I feel kind of-- *faint*.

Mark, you're *disappearing*!

MARK!

SOMEWHERE ELSE...

Abby, I-- hey! Where am I?

What? *Who* got me?

He got *you*, too? Well, *welcome* to the *party*.

I did. I am the *Game Keeper*. One of yours *transgressed* into my dimension and made me *aware* of the champions of Earth.

I require *entertainment* and *sport*. Thus, I shall pit you against your *opposites* to see who is stronger.

All games require a *boon* to the *victors*. So, you will compete not only for *your* freedom, but for the freedom and life of the *trespasser*.

I keep *telling* you: I *wasn't* trespassing. My dimensional portal *malfunctioned*!

Just *had* to mention *Crisis Season*, didn't you?

Sorry.

BACK ON EARTH...

I talked with Paul's housekeeper. She says that he *vanished* right in front of her, too.

So, *wherever* they are, they're *probably together*.

That's *good*.

Now we have to figure out how to solve *my* problems.

What?

Your fiancé and *my* friend both vanish--

--pulled off to *who knows where*--

--and you're worried about *your* problems?

Charlotte, it's *not* like this is the first time something like this has happened to *either* of them. They'll handle it.

Meanwhile, *I'm* an *American citizen* in a *foreign country* with *no passport* and *no record* of crossing the border.

We've got to handle the things we *can* handle.

Besides, worrying about *me* keeps me from worrying about *him*.

MEANWHILE...

Heroes of Earth. You may *take quarter* on this planet until you are *each* called to do battle with your foe.

Lovely.

I'll go *search*--

You'll do *nothing*, yet. Crusader--?

Looks like we're in the *Alpha Tauri system*, so that puts us about *65 light-years* away from Earth.

There's a pretty strong *force field* around the planet, too. We're *stuck*.

Okay, Blurstreak, *now* you can do some recon. We're looking for some sort of *focus* for Game Keeper's power.

Until *then*, we're going to have to play *his* game. Keep *sharp*, people.

So an omnipotent godlike being has nothing *better* to do than to make us play *Super Hero Survivor*?

The siren call of *reality television* apparently knows no bounds.

PARIS, FRANCE...

I *don't* want to make the call.

Abby, you *have* to.

You said Mark *gave* you that number just in case anything *like this* ever happened and you couldn't reach *Paul.*

Go ahead and make the call. I'll go make some more *tea.*

You have anything *extra* you can put in that?

I think I can find *something.*

CHARDON, OHIO...

A phone call during *breakfast?* That's *never* good.

Nope.

RIIING!

ELSEWHERE-

Darkblade's going to be upset that you're *stealing his act.*

The *brooding.*

Hmmm... what?

Oh. I'm just feeling *stupid,* I guess.

You're *not* the first one of us who someone got the *drop on.*

Arachnerd, you are *called...*

It's not *that,* Mark. While Game Keeper had me as his captive, I had a lot of time to *think.* And I'm *sorry.*

Zoe, I *just said* that we've *all*--

No, *Mark*--

--I'm sorry about *writing that book.*

Mark, I understand *now* how that book hurt you and Abby. And I'm *sorry* for that. It's *part* of why I've been avoiding you lately.

Part of--?

I *was* captured by a blue-skinned alien game nut, a week ago, too. Did you *miss* that?

Oh, *yeah*.

And that's the other part. Game Keeper let *me* choose *which* of Earth's champions played for *my* freedom.

You were my first choice. If I had to gamble my life on *anyone*, it'd be you.

But then I wondered if you would have *chosen* to come.

I can take a *lot* of things, Mark.

But I can't take losing my *friend*.

He's right here.

MEANWHILE...

Mark's Dad is leaving for Deco City *now*. He'll get to your apartment around 4:00pm our time.

With the time change and all, that should leave him *plenty* of time to FedEx your passport tonight.

Mrs. Spencer, there's *no way* I can thank the two of you enough.

You don't have to. You're *family*. That comes with *crisis service* and the *recipe* to Grandma Spencer's delta bars.

Does this ever get any *easier*, Mrs. Spencer?

Easier? Oh, heavens, *no*.

You just get more people to *share it* with.

52

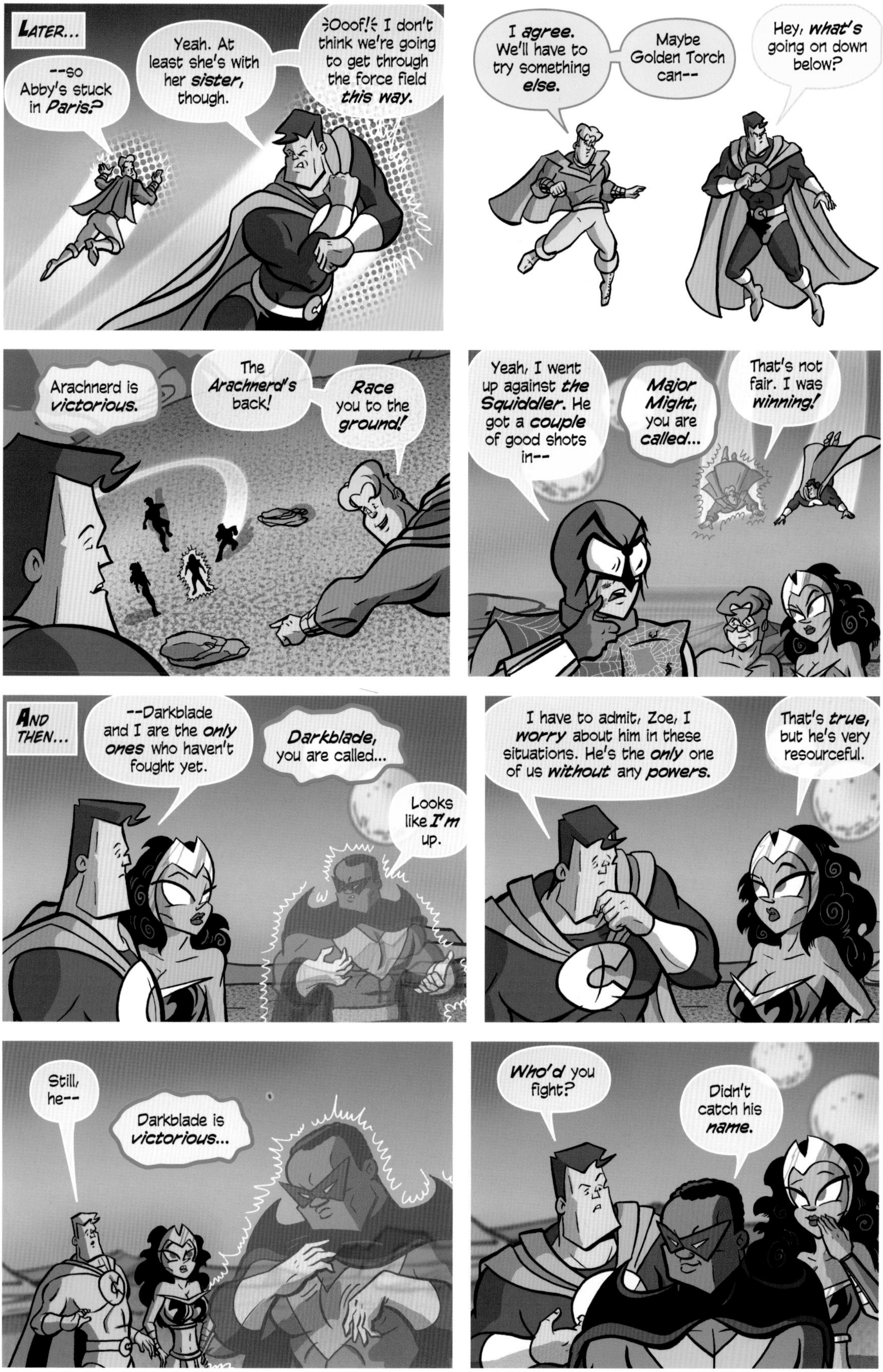
LATER...
--so Abby's stuck in Paris?
Yeah. At least she's with her sister, though.
Oof! I don't think we're going to get through the force field this way.
I agree. We'll have to try something else.
Maybe Golden Torch can--
Hey, what's going on down below?
Arachnerd is victorious.
The Arachnerd's back!
Race you to the ground!
Yeah, I went up against the Squiddler. He got a couple of good shots in--
Major Might, you are called...
That's not fair. I was winning!
AND THEN...
--Darkblade and I are the only ones who haven't fought yet.
Darkblade, you are called...
Looks like I'm up.
I have to admit, Zoe, I worry about him in these situations. He's the only one of us without any powers.
That's true, but he's very resourceful.
Still, he--
Darkblade is victorious...
Who'd you fight?
Didn't catch his name.

CRUSADER'S TURN...

Hello, Crusader!

Psi-Clone?

That's right, Crusader. And it's time to *get even* for you putting me away three years ago.

You *really* think you can do that?

Not *me*--

--but *you*.

I've duplicated all your *powers* and *memories*, Crusader--

--or should I say *Mark Spencer?*

So you're *me*, eh?

Cool. It'll be nice to not have to *hold back* for once.

FINALLY...

Very funny.

Crusader? Who'd *you* have to fight?

Didn't catch his *name*.

Guys, I think *something's* happening.

Heroes of Earth--you have *won* the day.

The Game Keeper is a fair player. I *release* Amazonia and will *return you* to your points of *departure*.

I *thank you* for the entertainment.

From *this day forth*, enter my dimension *freely*.

At least he said *"thank you."*

PARIS...

Well, that should be the *last* thing. *Jason* will open up the store tomorrow.

And might I say that was a *very* convincing cough.

Well, I *have* done community theatre.

So I guess there's nothing left but the *waiting*.

Waiting for my passport. Waiting for *Mark*. Wait--

Um, Abby--

Charlotte, it's *bad form* to interrupt someone's *self-pitying spiral*.

Well, *go on* then.

I can *wait*.

AND THEN...

--so you *each* had to fight a super villain while he *watched* and *kept score?*

Pretty much.

And how did *my* fiancé do?

Oh, he *gave* as good as he *got*.

You know, we should probably be *heading home* if we're going to catch your Dad *before* he sends out my passport.

Good idea.

Goodbye, Abby. Glad you're *okay*, Mark.

Take care, Charlotte. We'll see you *soon*.

Any time, Abby--

--any time as long as you *remember your pass-port*.

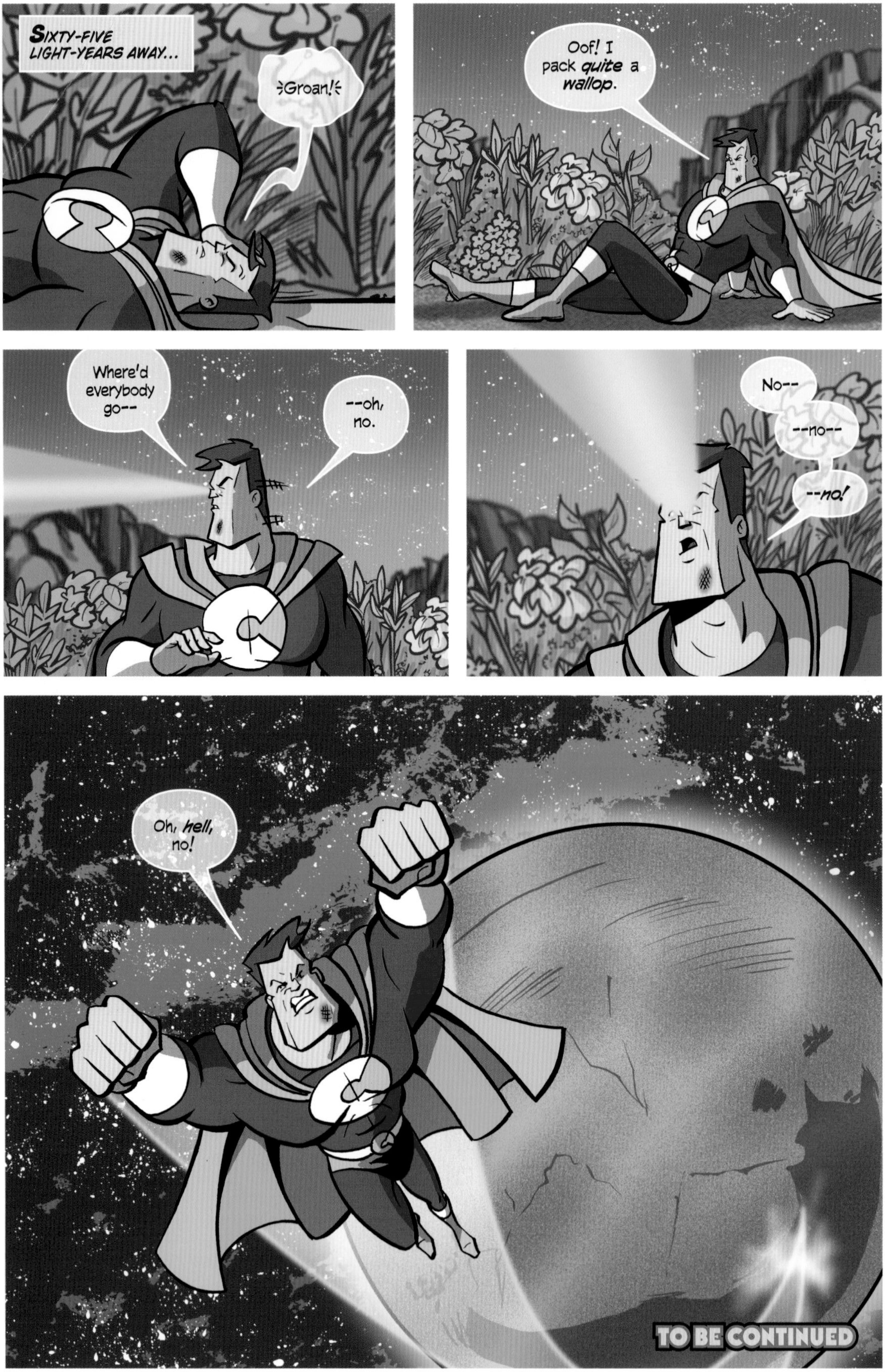
SIXTY-FIVE LIGHT-YEARS AWAY...
Groan!
Oof! I pack quite a wallop.
Where'd everybody go--
--oh, no.
No--
--no--
--no!
Oh, hell, no!
TO BE CONTINUED

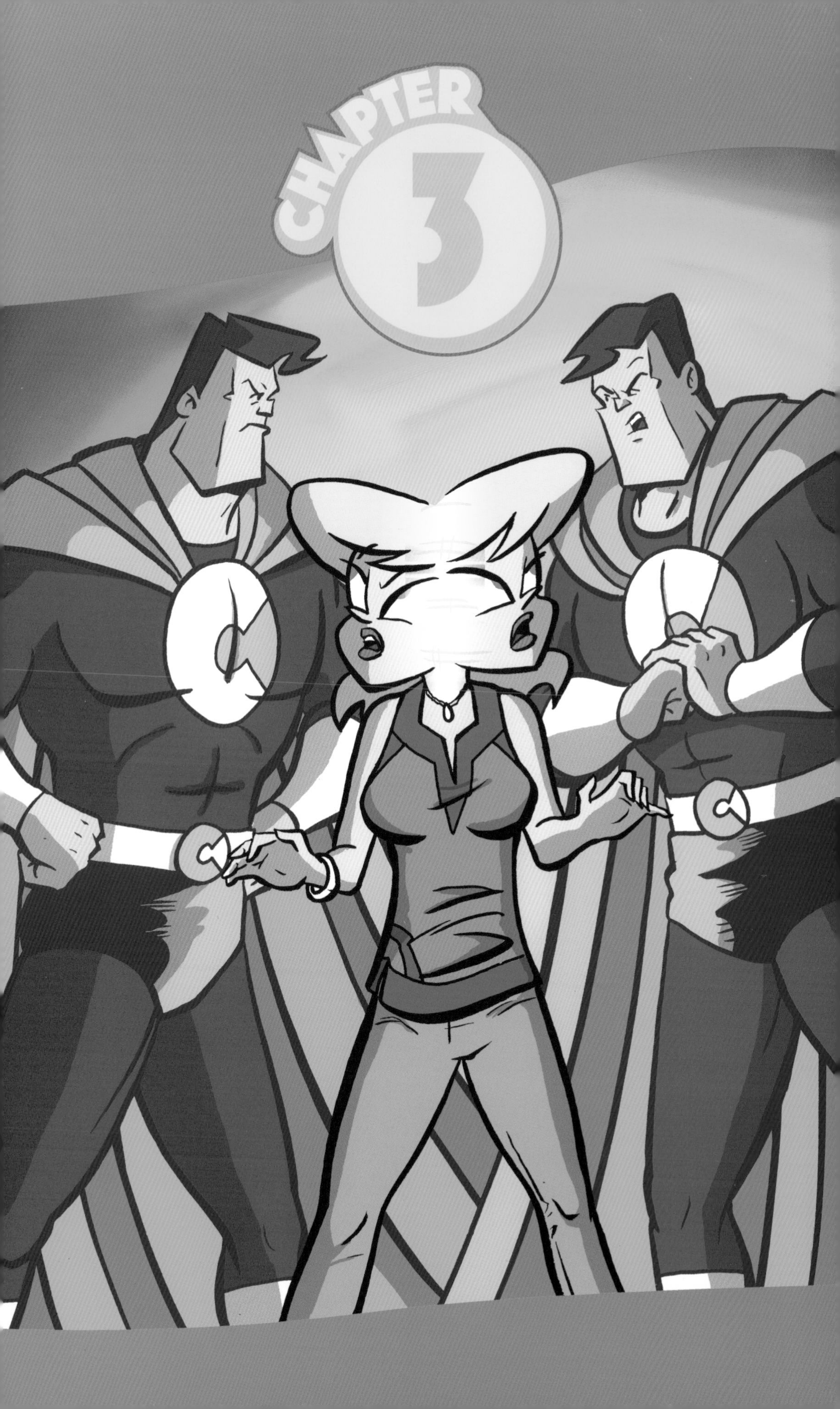
CHAPTER
3

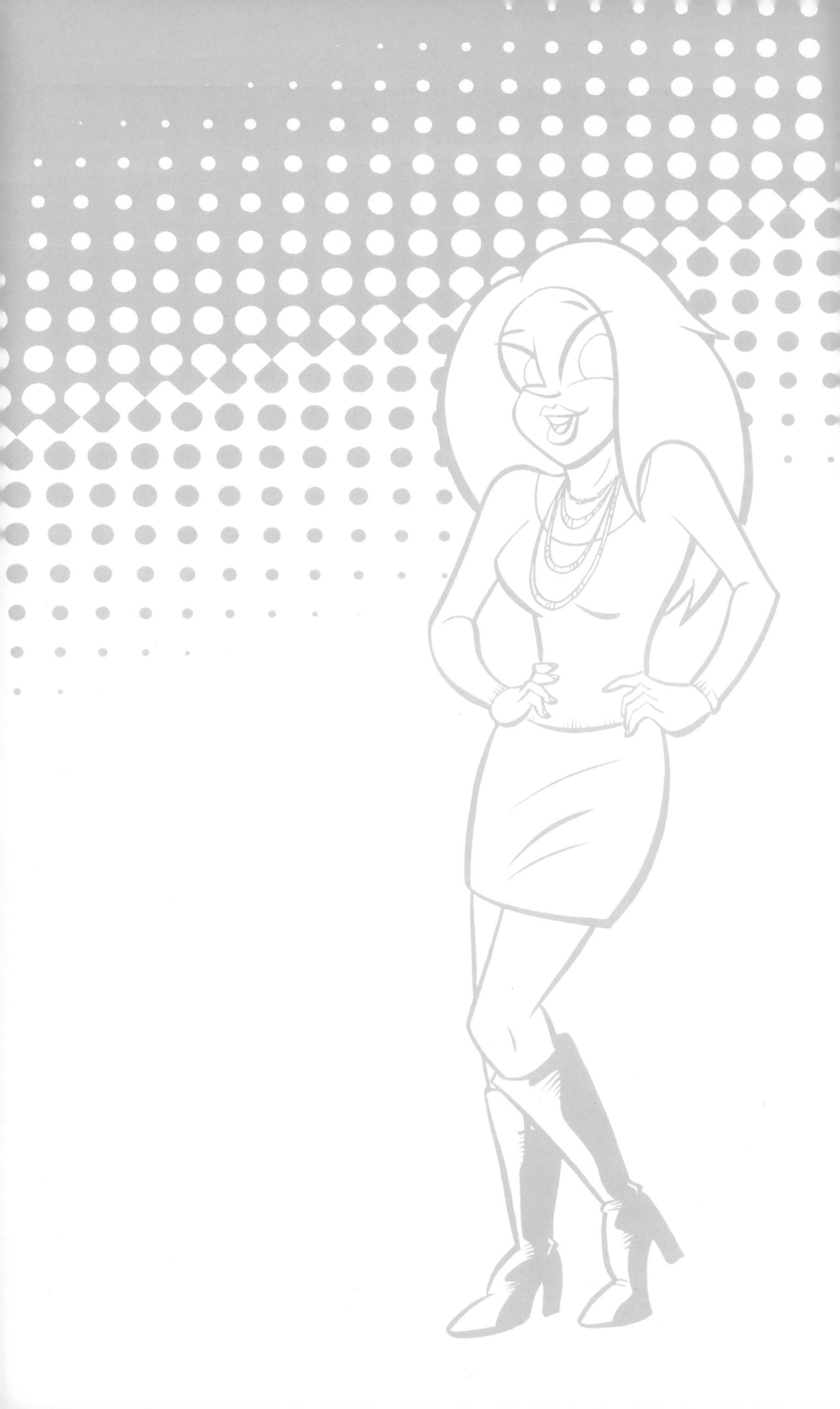

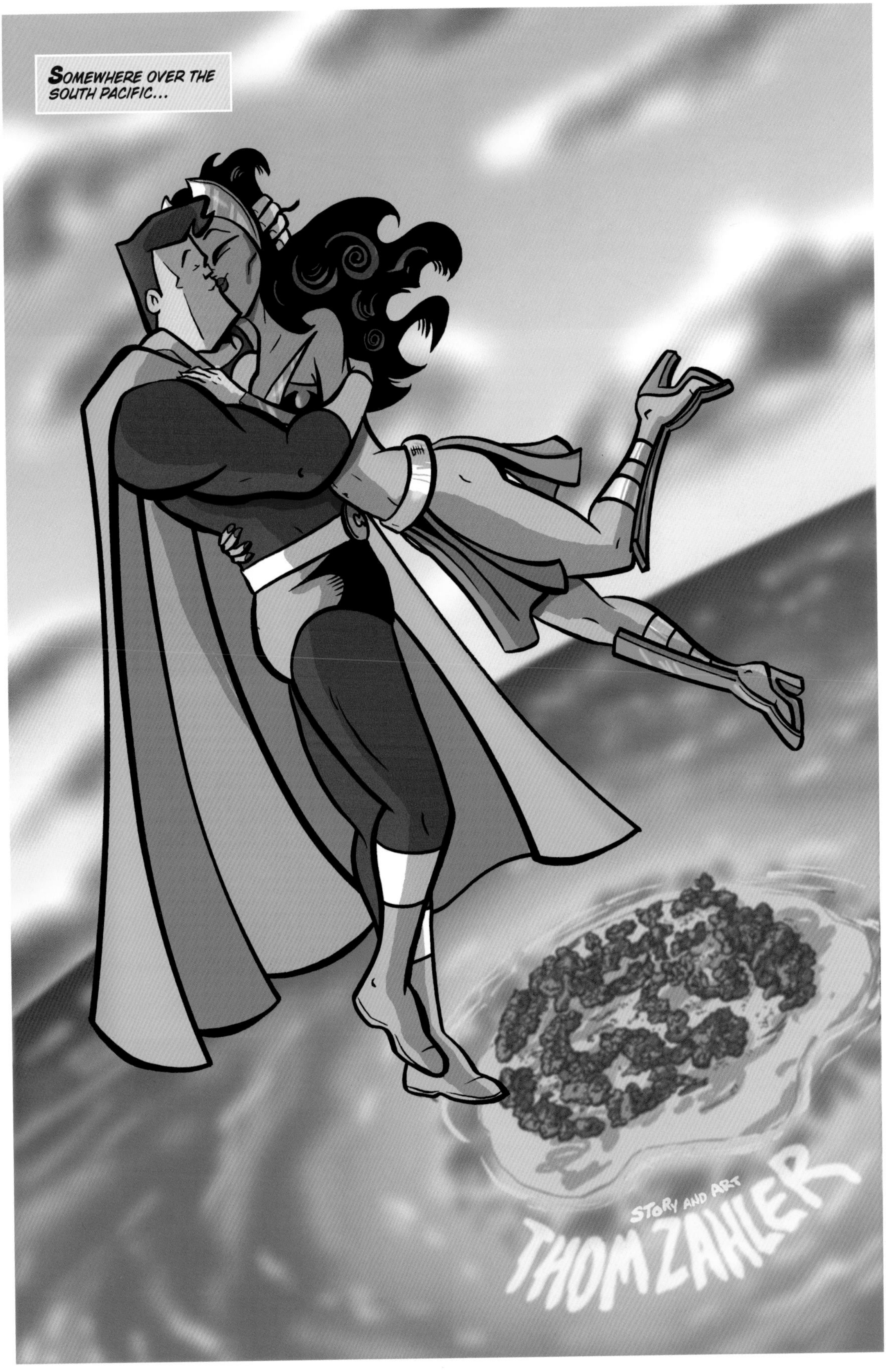
SOMEWHERE OVER THE SOUTH PACIFIC...
STORY AND ART
THOM ZAHLER

Left figure: I'm glad you could clear your *afternoon*.

Right figure: I'm glad you *suggested* it. You *know* I love the Tropics.

Left: Reminds me of that time we fought *Isle Robot*.

Right: Oh, *don't* remind me. A sentient mechanical island? What was the Evil Brain thinking?

Left: Well, that *was* in his wacky genius period.

Right: I think that was his last campaign before he switched to his *grim, tortured phase.*

Of course, not *all* change is bad.

I'm *not* complaining, but since we got back from that Game Master thing last week, *you've* certainly been *different.*

Oh, yeah. I feel like a *new man.*

Left: So when can we start *telling* people about us?

Middle: Um, well--

Right: Mark! We *can't* keep putting this off.

I understand that you don't want to hurt *Abby*, but you two *broke up*. It's *over.*

And I won't be your little secret *forever.*

Soon. I promise.

All right. I have to go. I've got a meeting with *Oprah* tonight.

Yeah, I've got an *appointment* myself. I'll *see* you--

Caption: LAS VEGAS...

--and *call.* Full house!

Man, it's like he can *see our cards!*

LATER, AT MARK'S APARTMENT...

You can go *anywhere*, do *anything*--

I tell you, Spencer, you don't know *how good* you had it.

--eat *any-thing* you want and *never* gain a pound--

--*drink* as much as you want--

--of course, the whole *invulnerability* thing spoils that one a bit.

THEN...

Now the only question is what to do *next.*

More quality time with *Amazonia.* How you ever left *that* I'll never know.

Vegas was *fun,* but it loses a little of its charm when you *can't lose.*

I could *terrorize* some of my ex-partners--

BING-DOO-BEEP!

Sheesh! *Needy* much?

How *many* times a day does this chick call you, Spencer?

Ignore.

NOW CALLING
ABBY

IGNORE CALL

Well, that settles *that.*

I guess I really *will* have to *dump you* tomorrow.

THE NEXT DAY... --so, it seems like Mark's *avoiding* me. What do you think, Jason?

As long as my sister is in *Paris*, yes.

Is "relationship counselor" *really* part of my job here?

Really, Abby, I'm *not* very good at this.

I just need someone to help me *figure this out.* He's *not* acting like himself.

Fine. Well, let's see--

--has he ever kept *any secrets* from you before?

Um, secrets?

What's wrong?

You're right. You really *aren't* any good at this.

THEN... Looks like Mark's *finally* returning my call.

BING-DOO-BEEP!

Mark, honey? *Where* have you been? I haven't seen you in almost *two weeks.*

What? well, sure I--okay.

Bye. I *lo*--

So, *what* did he say?

Uh-oh. That's *never* good.

He said we need to *talk.* Tomorrow.

Coffee break *already?*

Yeah.

Let me know how the weather is in *Paris.*

LATER, IN PARIS...

--so you're just *waiting* on a rooftop for him?

Yeah. He said he wanted to talk *somewhere quiet.*

Abby, I *love* the guy, but this doesn't sound good.

I know.

Maybe it's just that whole *life of a superhero thing.* It could be really busy--

Abby, I don't care *who* he is or *what* he does, he *doesn't* get to treat my sister like this.

You *tell* him I think he's being a--

Charlotte *knows* I can hear her, right?

I think she's *counting on it.*

Mark, I know *something's* wrong, but *whatever* it is, we can work through it.

Abby--

Mark, I love you more than *anything*--

Abby, don't--

Look, things have *changed* with me. I'm *not* the same person you fell in love with.

And I--

This shouldn't be so hard.

What, Mark? *What* shouldn't be so hard? What are you *trying to say?*

I think we *both* know--

63

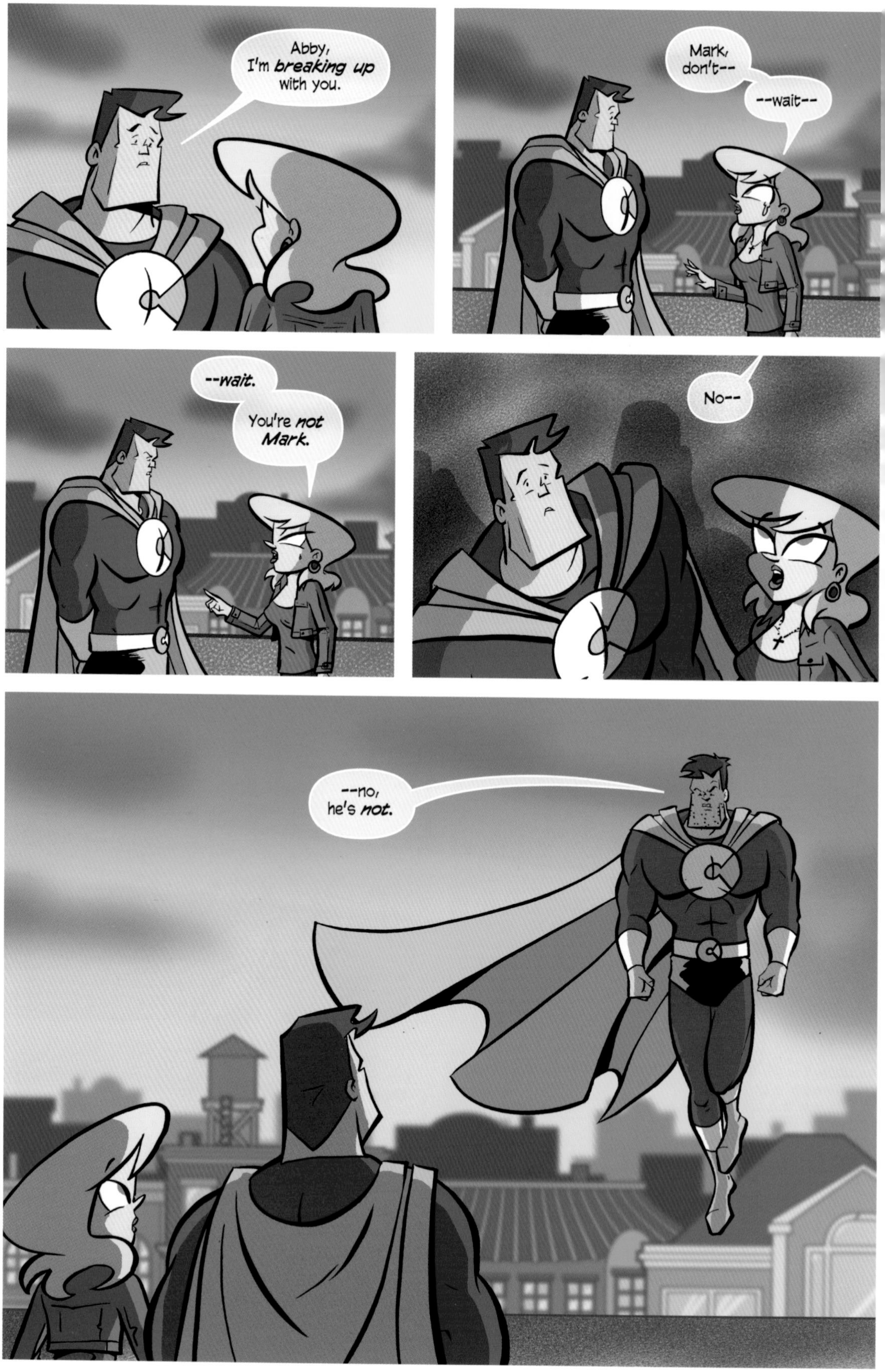
Abby, I'm *breaking up* with you.
Mark, don't--
--wait--
--*wait.*
You're *not Mark.*
No--
--no, he's *not.*

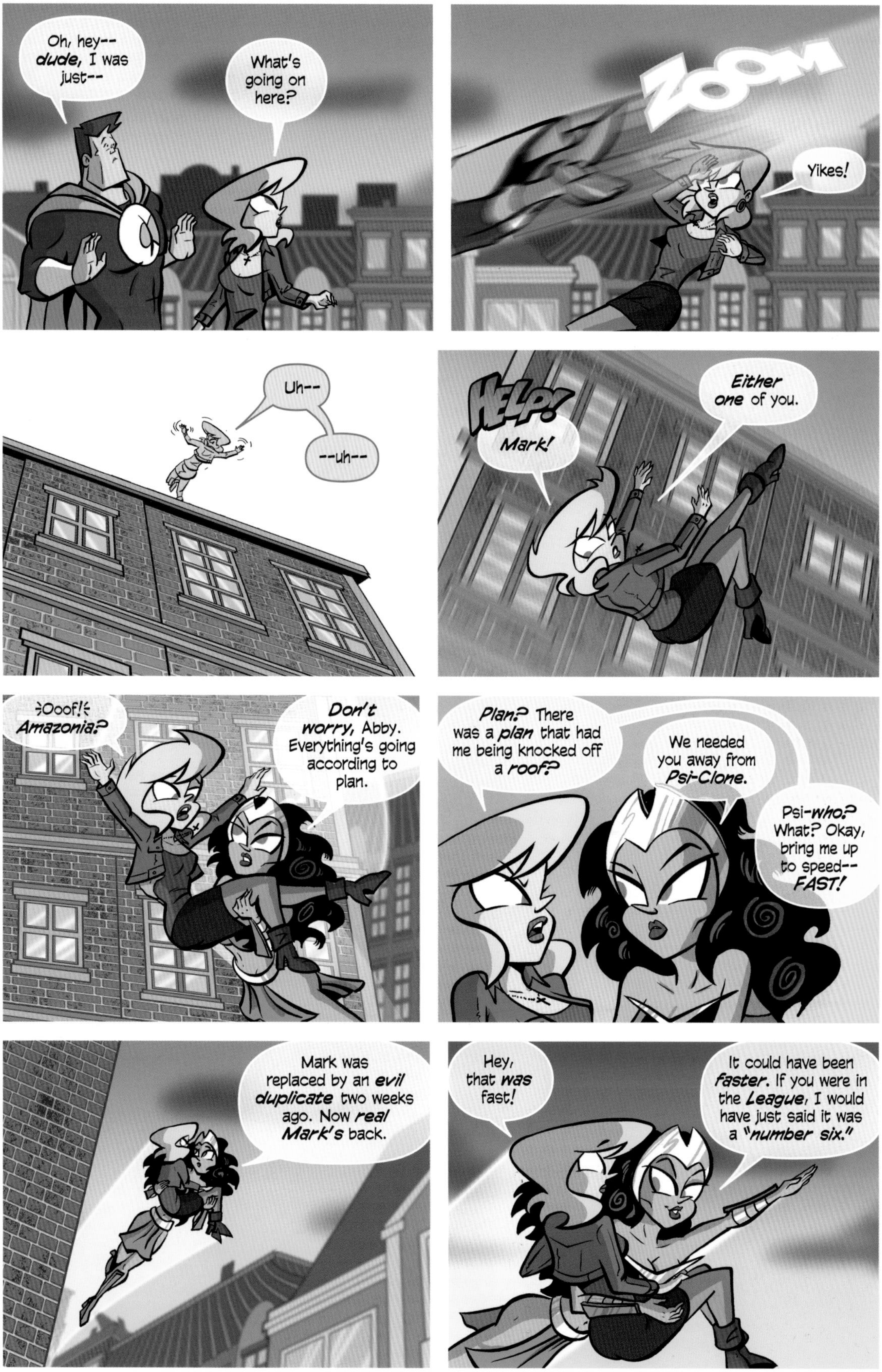

Oh, hey-- dude, I was just--
What's going on here?
ZOOM
Yikes!
Uh--
--uh--
HELP!
Mark!
Either one of you.
Ooof!
Amazonia?
Don't worry, Abby. Everything's going according to plan.
Plan? There was a plan that had me being knocked off a roof?
We needed you away from Psi-Clone.
Psi-who? What? Okay, bring me up to speed-- FAST!
Mark was replaced by an evil duplicate two weeks ago. Now real Mark's back.
Hey, that was fast!
It could have been faster. If you were in the League, I would have just said it was a "number six."

Why are we going *here?*

It's part of the *plan.* Mark told me to bring you here.

So, who is that guy *impersonating* Mark?

His name is *Psi-Clone*--

--he wears a *shape shifting harness* that allows him to duplicate other people's forms *and* memories.

He *switched places* with Mark back on that Battle World--

BOOM!

BOOM!

Is that thunder?

No--

BOOM!

--but a storm *is coming.*

BOOM!

THEN...

Shouldn't you be doing something to *help?*

WHAM!

Change back!

No, he said to *stay out* of it.

He wanted us to just *stand around* and *watch?*

Make me.

For now. He said it was *important* that you see this.

Oh, that one looked like it *hurt.*

Please. *I've* hit him harder.

Yes, but *he* didn't just drink the *last* Frappucino in the League fridge.

Hey, I was *saving* it for later.

You *found* it?

Yeah, it was in Professor Deuterium's old lab. In *pieces*, but I can fix *that*.

I'll be glad when this is over. I *hate* shape shifters.

Darkblade! ⹃Pant!⹄ Glad you made it. ⹃Huff!⹄ Now *blast* him!

Wait? Blast *me?* *No*, blast *him!*

Oh, *come on!*

Man, I *really* hate shape shifters.

And so...

Okay, we clearly have a *standoff* here.

So, to *whichever* one of you is my *best friend...* I'm *sorry.*

And to whichever one of you is *Psi-Clone...*

...I hope this *hurts.*

What *is* that?

It's an *omni-directional hypersonic emitter.* To people like you and me, it's nothing--

But to people with *super hearing,* it's like *nails on a chalkboard* in their *skull.*

Or a *Celine Dion* concert.

Gah! What are you *doing*? This will *kill* us!

If *that's* what it takes.

But I *don't* *want* to change back!

You're *serious*, aren't you? You'd *really* go through with this?

You've got *my memories*. So you should know--

--exactly *how far* I'd go to protect *her*.

꿁Sigh!꿁

Just don't hit me *too* hard.

Deal.

Thwap!

Headache?

Just a *huge* one, yeah.

Thanks for doing that, buddy. I know it *wasn't* *easy.*

Glad to have you back, Mark.

Good to *be* back. Now, if you'll *excuse* me--

--there's *someone* I've been *dying* to see.

68

Sorry I'm *late*.

I'm just glad you made it *at all*.

You know, I'm not usually the *mushy type*, but they are a *really sweet couple*.

Oh, yeah. *Adorable*.

Let's get up to the satellite.

THE LIBERTY LEAGUE SATELLITE...

--so after a few hours I found a passing *Vogon cruiser*. They don't normally take *hitchhikers*, but I *did* save their planet from a Nova Bomb.

They got me to *Hak'tyl* a week and a half later and from there I hopped the *Stargate* to Earth.

Can you hand me my *uniform?*

Here it is, *washed* and *ironed*.

I can't tell you *how much* I've been dreaming of a *shower*.

The Vogons have a *mud bath* with dirt eating bacteria, but I couldn't bring myself to use it.

I can understand *that*.

And shaving. God, I missed my *atomic razor*.

Yeah. *Indestructible beard stubble* is no fun for *anyone*.

THE LIBERTY LEAGUE ARMORY...

That's the *source* of all our recent problems: the *Chameleon Harness.*

I wanted to make sure you knew it was *locked up.*

Thanks.

Don't you have to turn it over to the *government* or something?

No, our *U.N. charter* gives us a lot of flexibility with *Weapons of Super Powers.*

It's the same way we can keep Psi-Clone in one of our *holding cells* until his *memories fade.*

Without that harness, he'll forget *everything* about the last two weeks.

So *your secret* is safe.

Honey, we're going to be *married--*

--it's *our* secret now.

THE LIBERTY LEAGUE COMMISSARY...

Two weeks eating just *grub worms?* Heck, *I* might have hit a Burger King before I came to rescue me.

Don't think I didn't *think* about it.

Ding!

Sorry about not being able to let you in on our plan with Psi-Clone, by the way. I was afraid he might be *keeping tabs* on you.

No, I think he was trying to *stay away from me* as much as he could.

I know he had my memories and all, but *none of you* had *any clue* that he wasn't me?

I think I knew *something* was wrong, but "*evil duplicate*" wasn't on my list of possibilites.

He stayed away from *me,* too.

Uh...

Hey, is that the *Danger Alert?*

We need to *talk*, Psi-Clone--

Yeah, I had a *feeling* you'd be in to see me.

You want to know what *I* did when *I* was *you*.

Seems you *know me* pretty well.

Until everything *fades*, yeah. Don't worry, I didn't commit any *major* crimes or anything.

I even *saved* a few people. I kind of *liked* being you. I just had a little more... *fun*.

And my girlfriend?

Annie? Audrey? I stayed *away* from her as much as I could.

When I copied your *memories*, I caught some of your *emotions*, too. It sometimes happens with incredibly strong feelings.

So I loved her--a *little bit*. I couldn't be around her, because I knew she wasn't *really* mine, but I didn't want to *hurt her* either.

Eventually, the *guilt* got me and I decided to *break up* with her.

I see. Anything *else* I need to know?

Well, you *might* want to stay out of *Vegas* for a few months--

Later...

Hey! I've been here for *hours!* Can I get something to *eat?* A *sandwich* maybe?

You called?

Uh-oh.

Let's be *clear:* You want me to lower this *protective force field* that *separates* us so that I--

Um, you know what? Never mind. I'm not hungry anymore. Thank you, ma'am.

You'll let me know if you need anything *else?*

I'm fine. I think I'll just go back to *forgetting things* now.

THAT EVENING...

Abby, you're *early*--

And, um, are you wearing *that* to Chez Ferrer?

Well, I got to thinking...

After *two weeks away*, would you rather get *dressed up* and go *across town* to an expensive restaurant--

--or would you rather I *made* dinner and we spent the night clearing off your *TiVo* while you give your fiancee a foot massage?

I am a *lucky man* to have you, aren't I?

Yes, you *are*.

Wait--*foot massage?*

Can't be *all* about *you*, Spencer.

LATER...

You're *sure* you're okay with this? I mean, you *hate* this show.

It's fine, Mark.

Besides, if it means having you--the *real you*--back, then I'd sit through a *marathon* of this.

Previously on *Battlestar Galactica*...

Just to be clear, though, this *isn't* a marathon, right?

Nope. Just the *one*.

72

THE NEXT EVENING...

So, are you *settling back in* okay?

Yeah. Psi-Clone didn't do *too much damage,* fortunately.

He *did* try to hide some of his Vegas winnings.

I figured he'd use my super powers, not that he'd use my *accounting skills.*

Other than *that,* it's just been getting back into the *swing of things.*

And planning the *wedding.*

Which brings me to something I've been meaning to ask you--

--will you be my *Best Man?*

Mark, I'm honored--

Great, I--

--but *no.*

What?

Mark, I'd *love* to be your Best Man, but I *can't.* And *you know* it.

I *do?*

Look, you're *my* best friend--

--but Mark Spencer *isn't* Paul Lacroix's best friend.

How would you explain a *nondescript accountant* in Deco City being that tight with *"the Boy Mogul"?*

But *you* went out with *Charlotte*--

Right. But Paul Lacroix meeting a pretty girl *doesn't* require a cover story. Becoming *her sister's boyfriend's Best Man* is something else entirely.

Look, I'll *be there,* either in disguise or as Charlotte's date. We've got enough cover for that. Anything *else,* though, and we risk exposing our *secret identities.*

You know, sometimes this double identity thing really *bites.*

Look on the bright side: you've got an *iron clad reason* not to invite *Amazonia.*

73

THEN...

So? How did it go? Was Paul thrilled?

Not so much. He said "no".

You're kidding!

Nope. He was worried about the secret identity thing, and honestly, he's right.

But, when I was flying back, I had a thought--

If we moved the wedding back a couple months to Halloween, we could do everything in costumes and masks.

A...costume party...wedding?

Psych!

Seriously, though, Paul did say "no."

What's the deal with the envelope?

Oh, that? It's from Paul.

He likes to think he's four steps ahead of everyone, so sometimes he writes down predictions for me to read later to prove he called it right.

We started doing it after the third TV cliffhanger he spoiled for me.

He gave me this one and told me to open it when my "blood pressure spikes."

That's kind of fun.

Actually, I think it's just him showboating.

Really? I never got that vibe from him.

You've never seen him posing in front of a clocktower.

THEN... --we could rent out the *County Courthouse* for the reception. It's got that *huge* atrium.

I don't know.

But it looks *really cool.* All that *art deco architecture*--

You just want it because then you could say the reception was at "*The Hall of Justice.*"

Look at this place. It's the *University Club* downtown. *Very* swanky.

Oh, sorry. This *won't work.*

Why not?

No *rooftop access.*

⸮Sigh!⸮ This would be easier if I was just marrying *George Clooney* like I always intended.

Have you had that *wedding book* for a while?

Oh, yeah. I've been tossing ideas in it for *years.*

Any *dresses* in there?

Hey! Hands *off,* buster!

SMAK

Abby, they're just *pictures!* They're not even the *final* dress. Are you *that* superstitious?

On *this,* yes I am.

You know, a quarter inch of laminated cardboard can't stop me from *peeking.*

Maybe *not,* but I think my *wrath* will.

79

AND SO... I should probably be getting *back* to work.

Yeah, me *too.*

Psi-Clone wasn't exactly *keeping up* with all my accounting clients.

Hey, I just had an *idea.*

There *is something* you could do to help me pick out my *dress.*

Really?

LATER... I have to say, Abby, this wasn't *exactly* what I had in mind.

Well *how else* was I going to get to *Paris?*

PARIS... Do you have your *passport* this time, Abby?

⸨Sigh!⸩ *Yes,* I do. But Mark promised me he wouldn't *disappear* this time either.

Well, aside from having to leave so *you ladies* can go *shopping.*

Someone's being *superstitious.*

He's *upset* he can't see the dress.

Come on Mark. It's not like *you're* not *superstitious* yourself.

You always wear the *same lucky outfit* to fight crime in.

What?

Same lucky--? It's not an *outfit,* it's a *uniform.*

Well, don't worry. I *love* a man in uniform.

Lucky me.

I asked a couple of the *local girls* at school to get some dress shop suggestions.

Great! Thank you.

I've got most of the *morning* free, but we'll need to stop by the *Louvre* while we're out, too.

Not that I mind, but *why?*

I've got a *paper* to write on one of the paintings there.

I love *visiting* with you, but I've got to keep up with my *work*, too.

That's *ironic.*

How is *that* ironic?

I used to say the *same thing* to *you* when you worked at the *bookstore*.

LATER...

Abby, I think you bought everything *except* a wedding dress.

There wasn't anything I liked. Besides, it's been a *rough month*. I'm entitled to a little *retail therapy*.

That's certainly *true*. How *are* you doing?

I think I'm *over* the weirdness of the whole *evil twin thing* for the most part.

I'm surprised by *Mark*, though. He was completely *unfazed* by it.

It was *just another day* in the life to him.

It kind of *was*. From talking to Paul I know they see the whole thing as just a *job*--

--with *long hours* and *crappy pay*.

Well, that's just being *self-employed*.

81

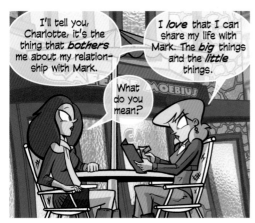

I'll tell you, Charlotte, it's the thing that *bothers* me about my relationship with Mark.

I *love* that I can share my life with Mark. The *big* things and the *little* things.

What do you mean?

But what it's like to be a *superhero*... that's the *one* thing we *can't* share.

I might be able to understand it *intellectually*, but I'll never *know* what it's like.

Well, I have some *bad news* for you then: that's *never* going to change.

You're just going to have to *accept* it.

Or go out and find a *radioactive insect* or *magic ring*.

...

Whoa! Why'd you stop?

I'm just thinking: *you're right*.

Of *course* I'm right.

What am I right about?

If I'm going to understand what Mark's life is *like*--

--I'm going to need to get some *super powers* of my own.

END

82

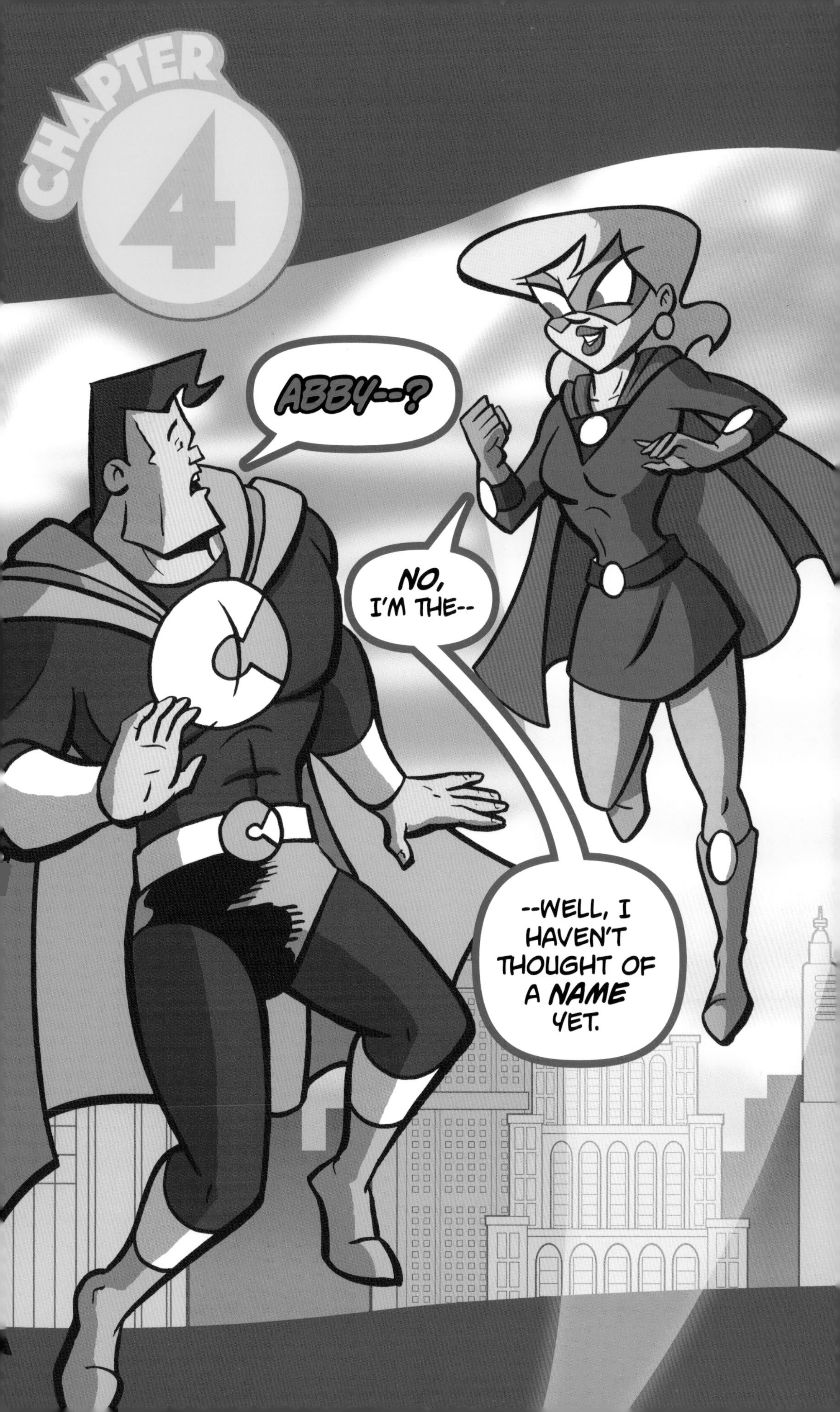
CHAPTER 4
ABBY--?
NO, I'M THE--
--WELL, I HAVEN'T THOUGHT OF A NAME YET.

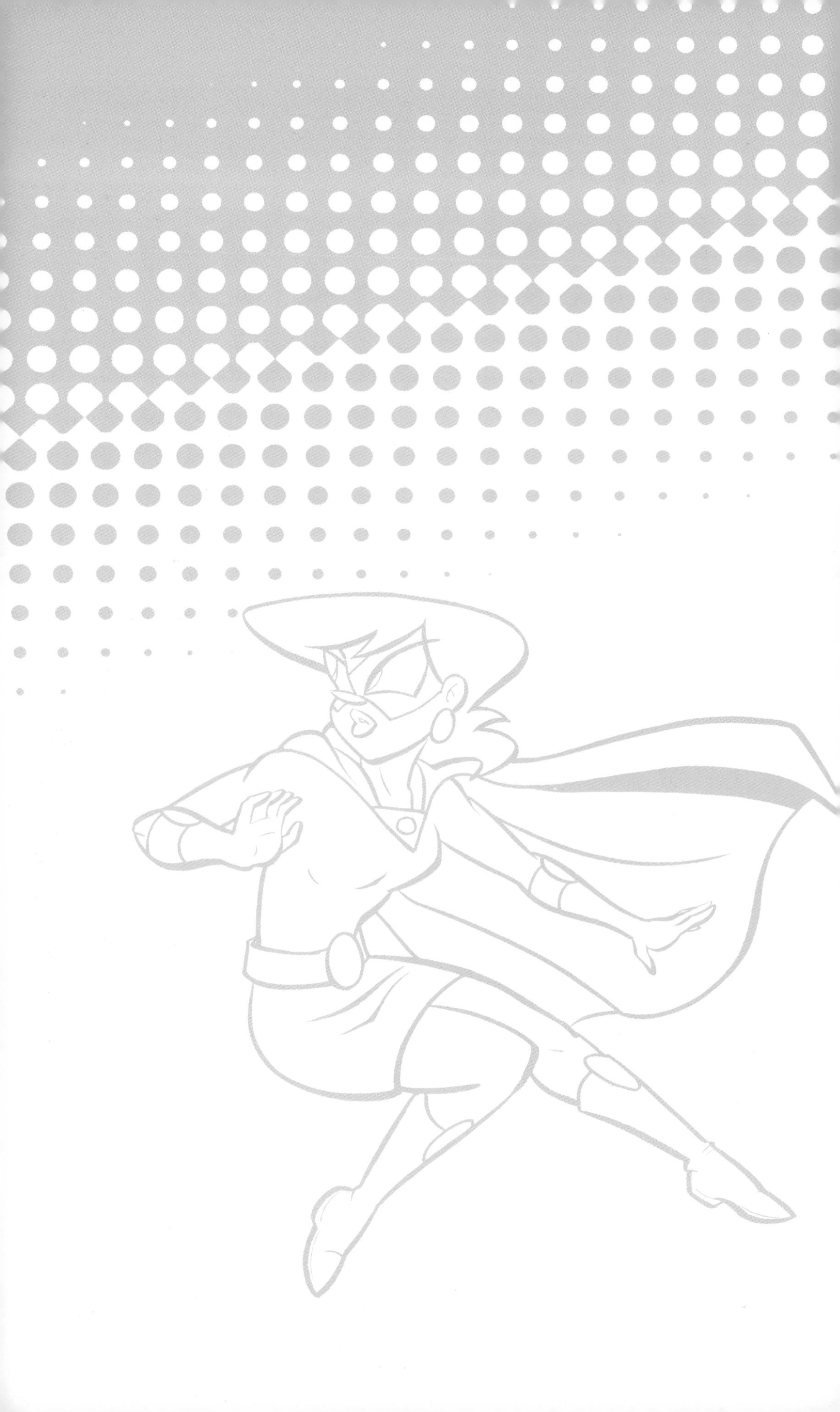

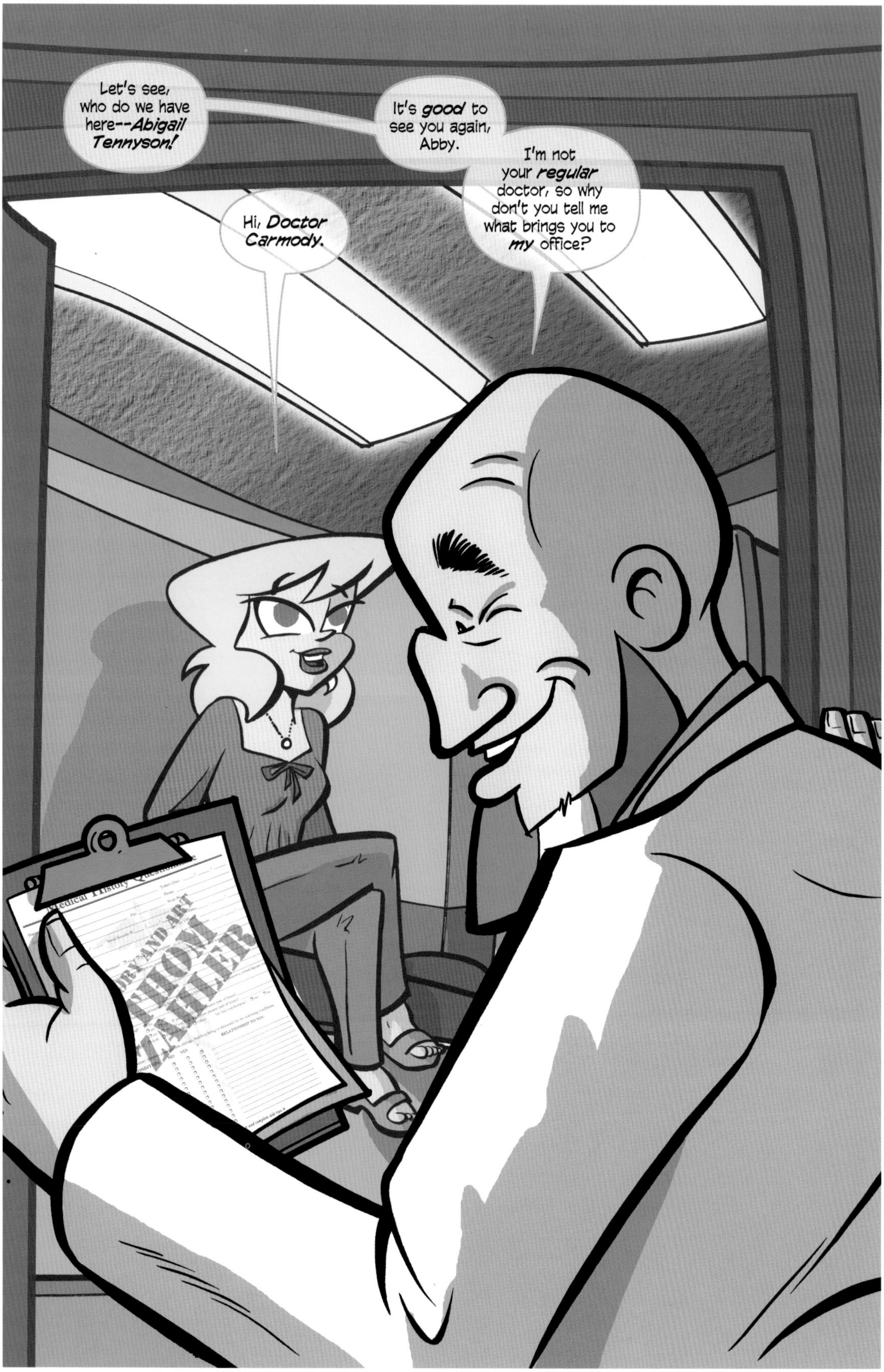
Let's see, who do we have here--*Abigail Tennyson!*
It's *good* to see you again, Abby.
Hi, *Doctor Carmody.*
I'm not your *regular* doctor, so why don't you tell me what brings you to *my* office?

It's a little complicated.

Mark always said if I had a...*super* problem I should see you.

In that case, there's *no need* to speak further--

--let me just do a *telepathic scan*.

But--

...er...

Still *can't read me*, can you?

Lords of Light! Women are *normally* complicated, but *you*...it's like a *maze* in there!

Why don't I just *tell* you why I'm here. It's kind of a *relationship thing*.

No, it's *nothing* like that. It's that... well, Mark and I are about to be *married* and *complete* each other's life.

I understand. I *am* a doctor.

Except that, for my part, I don't feel it *is* complete. I can never *really* be part of his life as the Crusader. And I really need to know what it's like, even if just for a *little while*.

You once *took away* his powers for a day. So, is it possible to give me powers *like* his for a day? Even an *hour?*

So can you *do* it?

Such a spell would require *powerful* magic and is not to be undertaken lightly

I'll need a *consult*.

How *long* will that--

--*take?!*

Just a *few* minutes. Why don't you wait here?

I'll have my *gargoyle* bring you some *tea*.

THEN...

--thank you for your *sage counsel*, Lady.

You are *most welcome*, Good Doctor. When next we meet, may it be in *person*.

So? Can you do it?

Aye, the Lady of the Flame allayed my *primary concern*.

A spell of this magnitude requires a *great source* of *power*

'Tis why such a spell often exacts a *high price*.

But you, fair Abigail, are doing this for *love*. And love itself is a *power* beyond *all reckoning*.

The lady reminded me that the *power of love* is *a curious thing*. It can make one man *weak*, and *another* one sing.

Do you find a lot of wisdom in the lyrics of *Huey Lewis and the News?*

The *Eighties* were a time of *great* cosmic awareness.

AND SO...

Abigail, while we have established that we *can* do this thing, we must now address *should* we do this thing?

How do you mean?

The mantle of a champion is a *heavy* one. I fear that you are *not aware* of its burden.

That's the *point*, isn't it? The only way to really understand it is to *experience* it.

I *bow* to your wisdom and logic.

Drink this elixir, and the spell shall be cast. Unless you have any *concerns*.

Just *one*. What does that stuff *taste* like?

I endeavored to enchant an aspect of *mint* to it. Be warned, though, that it may have a bit of a *kick*.

That should be *fine*. You never saw me in *college*.

The spell is **complete**.

I don't feel any **different**.

Shouldn't I **feel** different?

I thought I'd be able to see through stuff.

The spell is, at its heart, a **love** spell. While it is complete, it shall not activate **until** whence you next **kiss Mark**.

Then shall you have your powers.

Shall we now **away** to my office?

As always, it was a **true pleasure** to see you, Abigail.

Thank you **so much**, Doctor. I'll let you know how my **day** with super powers goes.

A **day**? Abigail--

--your powers are **not** so **chronally limited**.

They will last until such time as **you** decide you **no longer wish** to have **them**.

LATER...

Wait, so you could have super powers **forever?**

I guess so, Charlotte.

Oh God, you're going to be here in Paris **all the time**.

Don't worry, I promise **not** to abuse the privilege.

So, when's Mark coming over?

Actually, he should be over **any minute** now.

Do you know **how** you're going to tell him? Any **prepared speech?**

Or are you just going to meet him at the **front door** and say "Honey, guess what **I** did today?"

Not exactly--

--first, he doesn't **use** the front door.

Okay, Mark, I need to *tell you* something, and I need you to *promise* not to be mad.

Please tell me you *didn't* book that *ska band* for our wedding.

No, although I still think they'd be *great*.

Um, I kind of went to see *Doctor Karma* today--

--and had him cast a *spell* on me to *temporarily* give me powers just like yours. *Soon.*

WHAT? *Abby,* Why did you do that?

When do you *get* them?

Right now.

Oh--

--my.

Gah! There's so much...*noise*...so many...sounds!

It's *okay*, Abby. It'll be fine. Just *focus on my voice.*

Wha--? What are all those *squiggly things?*

They're just *radio waves*, don't worry.

Okay, I think I'm getting--

--getting *settled.*

--whoa! Are those *atoms?*

Good. Just take it *slowly.*

Hey! I can *totally* see through your *clothes!*

All right, that's *enough* of that.

Then...

Abby, I wish you had *asked me* before you did this.

But you would have told me *not to do it.*

Well, *yeah.*

Mark, being a super hero is the *biggest* part of your life.

If I'm going to be your *wife*, I think I need to know what that's like *firsthand.*

Besides, there's something you *haven't* considered.

Really? *What?*

I can *fly.*

You can *fly.*

WHOOSH WHOOSH

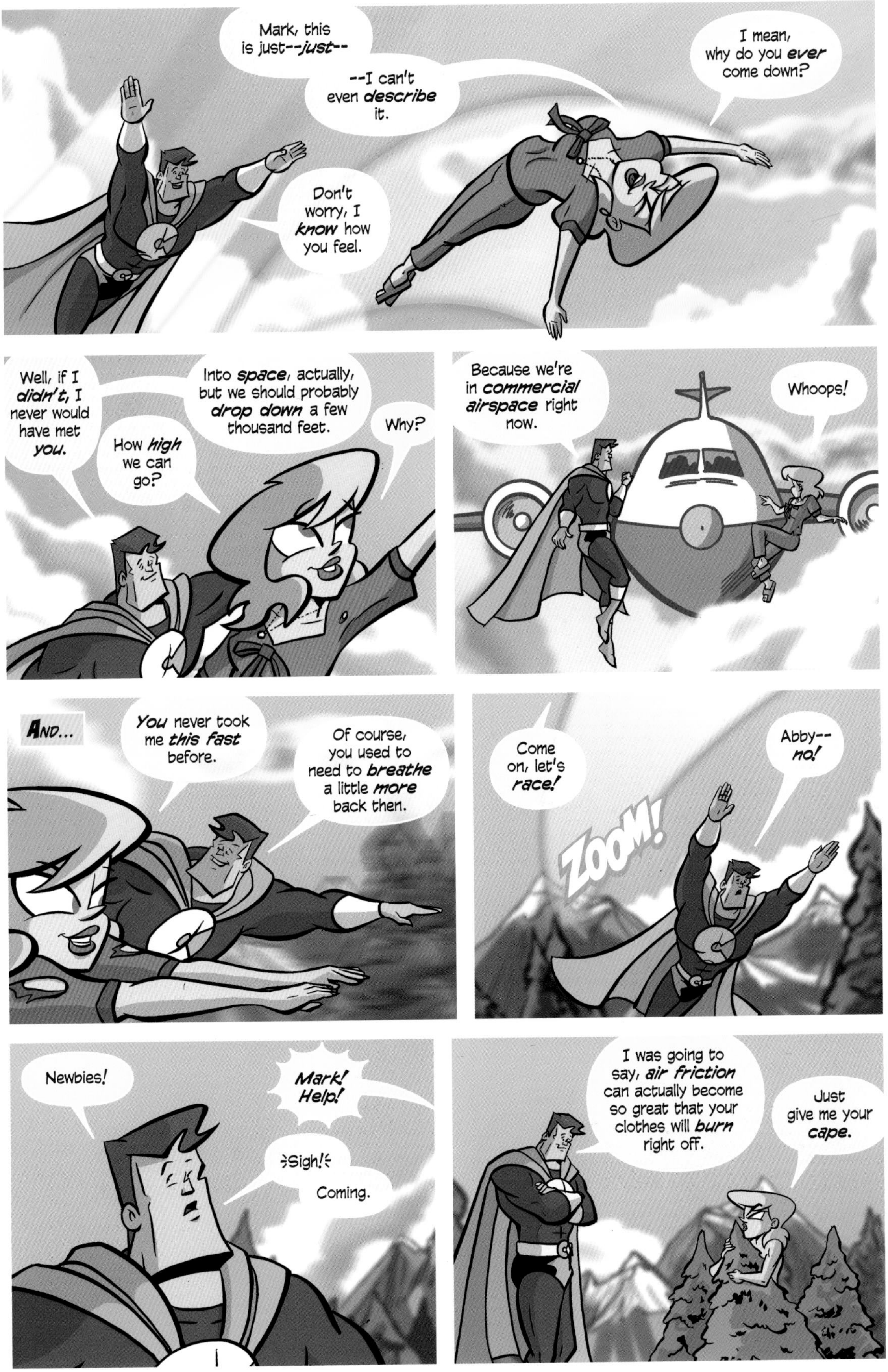

Mark, this is just--just--
--I can't even describe it.
I mean, why do you ever come down?
Don't worry, I know how you feel.
Well, if I didn't, I never would have met you.
How high we can go?
Into space, actually, but we should probably drop down a few thousand feet.
Why?
Because we're in commercial airspace right now.
Whoops!
AND...
You never took me this fast before.
Of course, you used to need to breathe a little more back then.
Come on, let's race!
ZOOM!
Abby--no!
Newbies!
Mark! Help!
Sigh!
Coming.
I was going to say, air friction can actually become so great that your clothes will burn right off.
Just give me your cape.

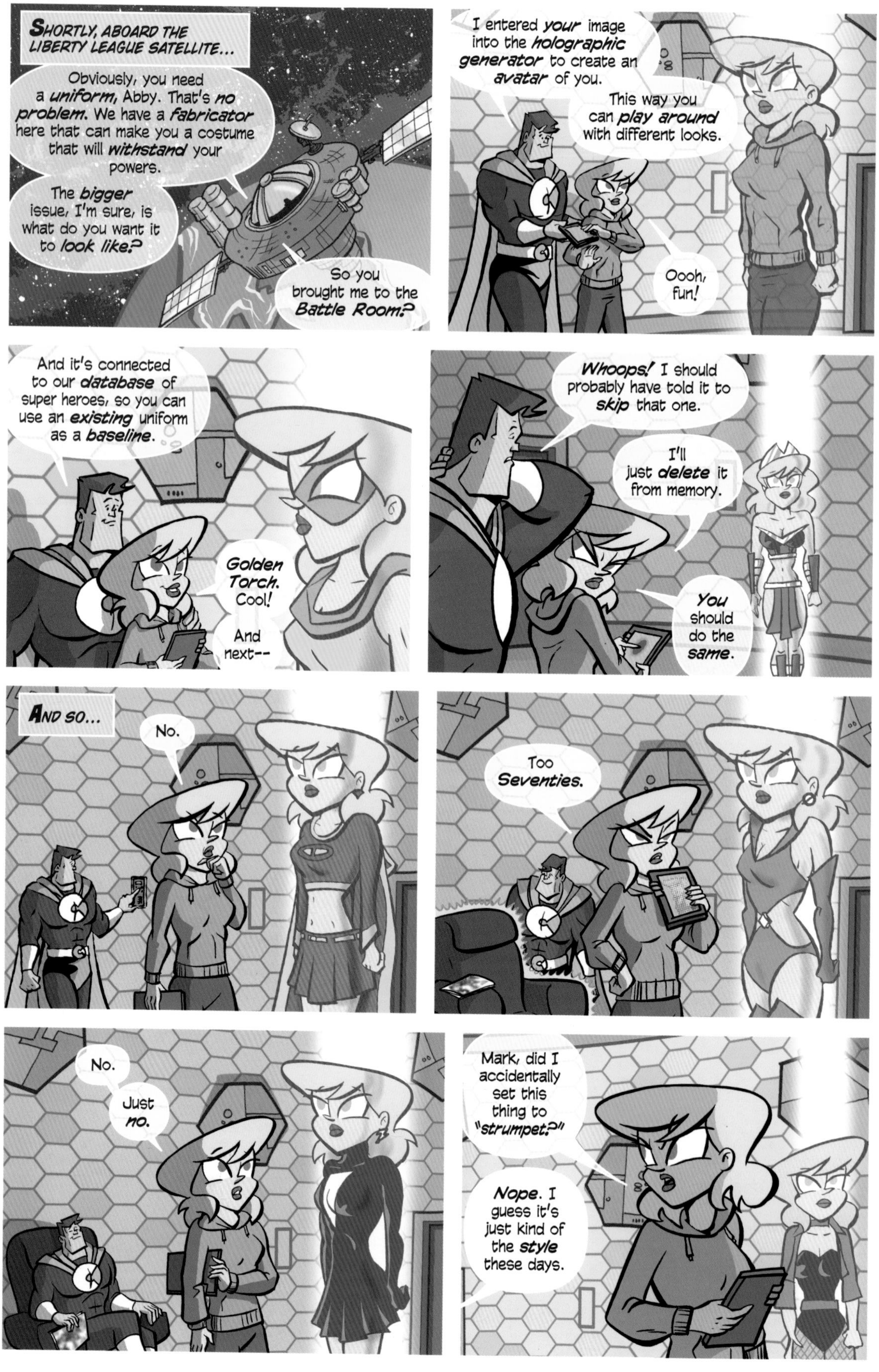
SHORTLY, ABOARD THE LIBERTY LEAGUE SATELLITE...
Obviously, you need a uniform, Abby. That's no problem. We have a fabricator here that can make you a costume that will withstand your powers.
The bigger issue, I'm sure, is what do you want it to look like?
So you brought me to the Battle Room?
I entered your image into the holographic generator to create an avatar of you.
This way you can play around with different looks.
Oooh, fun!
And it's connected to our database of super heroes, so you can use an existing uniform as a baseline.
Golden Torch. Cool!
And next--
Whoops! I should probably have told it to skip that one.
I'll just delete it from memory.
You should do the same.
AND SO...
No.
Too Seventies.
No.
Just no.
Mark, did I accidentally set this thing to "strumpet?"
Nope. I guess it's just kind of the style these days.

THEN...

And this **won't** hurt?

Not a **bit**. Only your **clothes** will be affected.

Okay, I've loaded your design into the fabricator. **Step in.**

How **long** will this--

ZAP!

Oh. That was **quick.**

Ta-da!

So you **did** go with a cape. You were on the **fence** about that before.

Oh, yeah. Capes are **classic.**

Plus it **covers my rear.**

That's why most of us wear them.

So what do **you** think?

Well--

Oh, God, you **don't** like it. It's the **colors,** right? They're super villain colors?

Or is it the **gloves?** I wasn't sure about those, but--

Abby! I **love** it. It just needs **one thing.**

What?

Gah! I am **such** an idiot!

Don't beat yourself up. Keeping your identity secret is an **acquired** skill.

MEANWHILE... Well, *this* visit is a surprise.

What do you mean, Paul?

I don't recall you venturing this far *north* before, Amazonia.

Liberty City does keep me pretty busy.

Still, can't a *friend* just drop by for a *visit?*

Of course. It's *always* good to see you, especially when it's *not* a crisis. But, I'm sure *something* motivated this visit.

Well, *yes.*

Mark always speaks *highly* of your *rooftop chats,* so I was hoping I could borrow you, too.

Mark also brings *coffee.*

⇃Sigh!⇂ You still take a *triple-shot espresso?*

ONE CUP OF COFFEE LATER...

So what's on your *mind,* Zoe?

I just didn't have anyone else to talk to about this. It's a *uniquely* super thing.

When Psi-Clone *replaced* Mark, he, um...

Rekindled your relationship?

You know, sometimes I forget how *good* a detective you *really* are.

Yes, that's *exactly* what he did.

And it kind of *reawakened* some feelings I thought I'd put to rest.

I know there's *nothing* I can do about it. Mark's *very* happy with Abby.

But still, I find myself *looking* at her and *wondering,* you know? I mean, I'm a *super hero* and she's just--

--just--

--Mark?

Hey, guys, didn't mean to *interrupt.*

I just thought I'd introduce you to Deco City's *newest* super hero.

Hi, guys!

Look who got herself *powers.*

Lord, I *hate* irony.

94

I'm going to guess that there's an *interesting story* here.

I guess. Abby wanted to know what it was like to be a *superhero*, so she got Doc Karma to *give* her powers like mine temporarily.

So we've got a *newbie* with *your* power set? Yeah, there's no way *that* could go badly.

She'll be *fine*. We've already talked, and she's not going to do too much without *me around*, just to be safe.

What have you *done* so far?

Not *too* much. Right now she's in the *experimenting* with her *powers* phase.

--I *still* don't see it.

It's right there *behind* that building--

Oh, sorry. I *forgot*. You don't *have* vision powers, do you?

LATER...

You know, I hadn't even *thought* about it.

Hey, Paul asked me a good question. What's your *code name* going to be?

How did *you* come up with *"Crusader"*?

It was my *grade school's mascot*. We were the *St. Mary's Crusaders*.

What was *yours?*

The *Cougars.*

Oh, well. We're probably a *couple* of years *too early* for that one.

⸼*Cough!*⸽ *"Couple?"*

THE NEXT MORNING...

Hey, honey. I thought I'd stop by and see how your *first super powered night* was and--

--what's wrong?

Oh, I started to look through some *books* to get an idea for a *code name.*

Then I realized how *fast* I was reading and *one book* lead to *another* and--

You read them *all.*

And now I have the informational equivalent of a *brain freeze.*

It's just that there were *so many books* I've always *meant* to read.

So I burned through the *Time Magazine 100 Greatest Novels List,* the *Modern Library* list...

...even *Oprah's* selections, God help me.

I'd take you to task for *abusing* your super powers if I hadn't done the *same* thing when I got mine.

And honestly, super speed was the *only* way I was ever going to get through *Finnegan's Wake.*

AND SO...

So, any *other* bumps on the *Super Brick Road?*

Just a little *sartorial* one.

Today's the *warmest* day in the last month, and I had the *cutest outfit* I've been *dying* to wear. But I *couldn't.*

No, I had to wear something *thick* and *long* sleeved so I could wear my costume underneath it.

So much for *short sleeves* and *skirts* while this experiment is going on.

Maybe if you picked one of those *trampier* costumes--?

Just *give it up,* Spencer.

Did you think of a name?

I was kind of thinking *Titania*. The Faerie Queen in Midsummer Night's Dream.

That's kind of--*hang on* a minute.

Good morning Mark, Abby.

Morning, Jason.

Is everything *okay?*

Yup.

If you say so.

You know, I do miss *Charlotte* every once in a while.

I under-stand.

THEN...

Whoa! Do you hear that?

A *bank alarm?* And sirens?

That's it. Come on, *let's go.*

Go? Mark, I'm *working.*

Oh, no. You wanted to know what it was like to be a *hero.* Abrupt absences are *part* of the *gig.*

But *what* should I tell Jason?

Clever excuses are the *hero's* problem, *Titania.*

Jason, I have to *step out* for a bit.

Okay.

All right, that just *wasn't fair.*

What can I say? It's *good* to be the *boss.*

97

SHORTLY...

Two perps—hang on. *Cancel* the SWAT team. *Big Red's* on scene.

Hi, *Sam.* What's the situation?

Two guys tried to hold up the bank. It went *south,* and everyone *got out.* But they're *holed up* in there and *armed.*

No problems there. Titania and I can handle it.

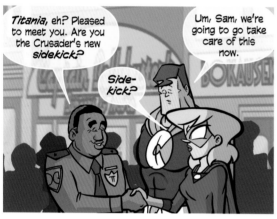

Titania, eh? Pleased to meet you. Are you the Crusader's new *sidekick?*

Um, Sam, we're going to go take care of this now.

Side-kick?

Sidekick?

Let it *go,* honey.

This is the Crusader! Come on out with your hands locked behind your head.

Otherwise, we'll have to come in there.

≶Sigh≷ Why do they *always*—

Dear?

BLAM!
BLAM!
BLAM!

You *do* remember that we're *invulnerable,* right?

Duh! I am such an *idiot.*

Don't beat yourself up. *Every-one* flinches the first time.

Come on. Let's go *bust some heads.*

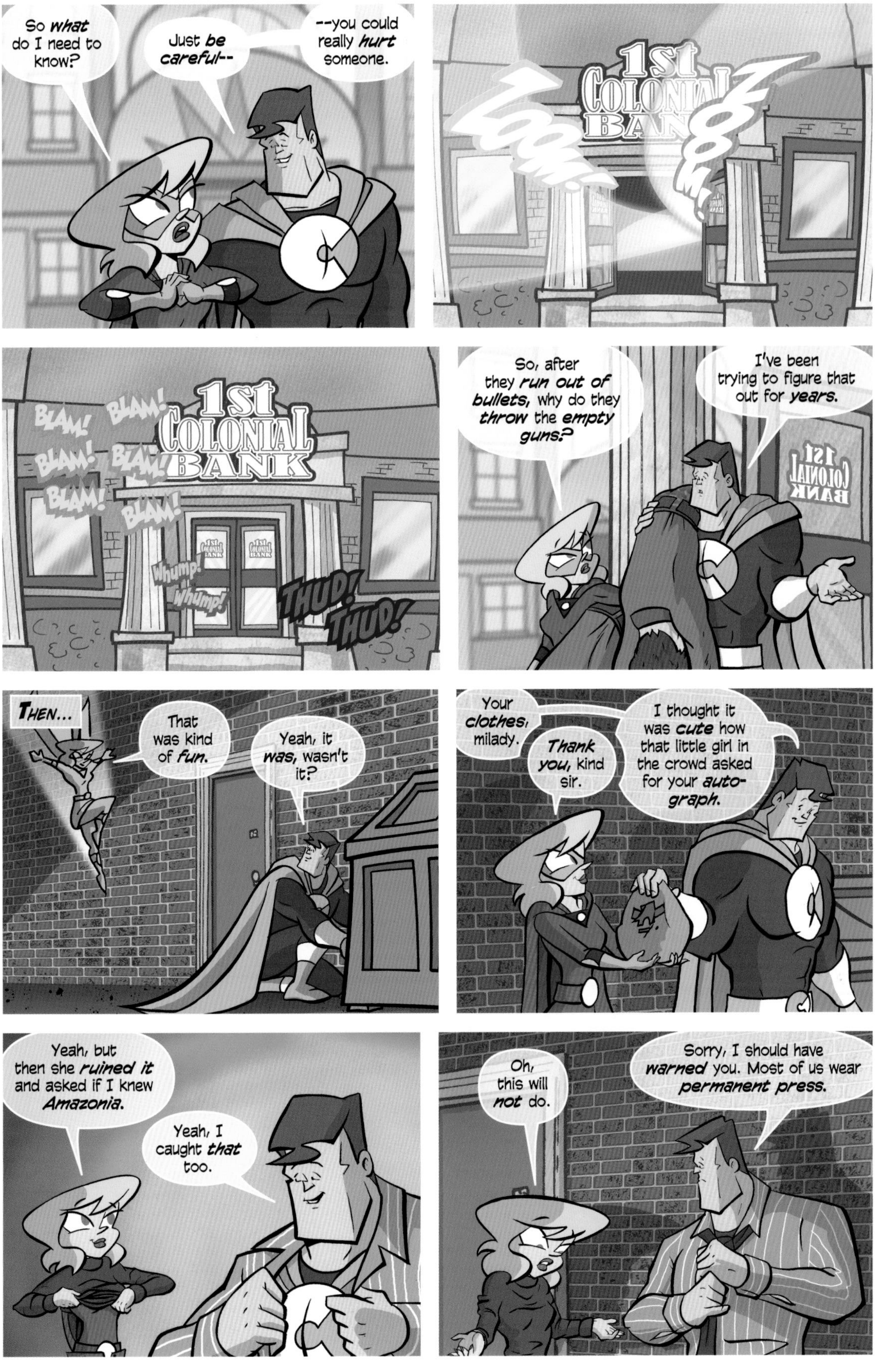

So what do I need to know?
Just be careful--
--you could really hurt someone.
1st COLONIAL BANK
ZOOM!
ZOOM!
1st COLONIAL BANK
BLAM!
BLAM!
BLAM!
BLAM!
BLAM!
BLAM!
Whump!
Whump!
THUD!
THUD!
So, after they run out of bullets, why do they throw the empty guns?
I've been trying to figure that out for years.
THEN...
That was kind of fun.
Yeah, it was, wasn't it?
Your clothes, milady.
Thank you, kind sir.
I thought it was cute how that little girl in the crowd asked for your autograph.
Yeah, but then she ruined it and asked if I knew Amazonia.
Yeah, I caught that too.
Oh, this will not do.
Sorry, I should have warned you. Most of us wear permanent press.

CHRONOPOLIS...

So how's Abby doing?

Good. I'm actually a little *surprised* how well. I *could* get used to this.

So *it* hasn't happened yet, has it?

It doesn't *have* to happen to everyone, Paul.

Don't *lie* to yourself, Mark. If she keeps her powers, it *will* happen.

I *know*.

It's what *I've* been worried about *all along*.

You want to talk about *something else?*

More than anything.

Where *is* the Most Powerful Bookstore Owner on the planet tonight, anyway?

She wanted to go visit her sister in *Paris*, so she's making her *first transatlantic* tonight.

Solo? Mark, the first time *you* went to Europe--

I *know*. I *tried* to tell her, but she wanted to do it *herself*.

You're a *cruel man*, Mr. Spencer.

Oh, my *cell phone* is ringing.

Whoever could it be?

BING-DOO-BEEP!

Okay, *fine*, you were *right*. I'm *lost*.

Not so easy *without landmarks*, is it?

100

PARIS...

Isn't Deco City the *other* direction?

Yeah, well, I got *turned around* a little bit.

Hello, Charlotte.

How are--

--you?

That's the look you went with? *Seriously?*

Nice to see *you*, too, Charlotte.

THEN...

So, you *have* to tell me. *What's* it like?

It's *complicated*.

It's *fantastic* being able to help and save people and stop crime. That's *all* good.

But, it's also like being on call *all the time*. No matter what you do, you can *never really relax*.

I don't think I realized what a *burden* it can be for Mark.

No, I meant what's it like having *super powers?*

Oh, that's *definitely* fun.

But it's always a bit of a *temptation* not to *abuse* them.

For instance, do I tell Mom you got a *tattoo* or do I just expect a *better birthday present* this year?

LATER...

My balloon!

See, I *told* you we should tie it to your wrist. Now, *next time* will you *listen* to *Mommy?*

Your mother's *right.*

I may not be around here to *catch* the *next one.*

Cool!

What's with *that* look?

I just think you're *adorable* is all.

AND THEN...

Is there anyone *still* in there?

I don't know. We *can't get in!*

Is that *every-one?*

Yeah. Let's go!

We can take her from here. *Thanks* for your help.

You're welcome. Now, if you'll *excuse* us...

SHORTLY...

Abby? Um, have you started *smoking?*

SNIFF! SNIFF!

AND THEN...

Mark, do you have anything for an *upset stomach?*

An upset--? Abby, you're *invulnerable* now. You shouldn't have stomach pains, or any *other* pains.

Unless...Abby is it a *dull pain* followed by lots of little *sharp pains?*

Yeah, that's it *exactly*. How did you know?

Suit up. We've got work to do.

Mark, *what's* wrong?

Our *super senses* are attuned to all *sorts* of things.

You *don't* have a stomach ache.

There's going to be an *earthquake.*

SECONDS LATER...

I didn't know that Deco City was on a *fault line.*

Not many people do. Heck, *I* only learned of it when I tangled with *Dig Doug* a couple years back.

It's largely *inactive*, but apparently *not today*.

You must have felt it *before* me because your powers are newer and you're a little more *sensitive.*

Whatever the reason, now we have to *stop it.*

Mark, *can* you stop an earthquake?

Depends. You remember that huge quake that hit LA last year?

No.

Then I guess I can.

The fault runs under the *park?*

Near it. But it's going to be easier to burrow through *this* than a *city street.*

Abby, I've called the Liberty League, but even at their *fastest* they won't be here for a couple of *minutes.*

I can stop the big quake, but there are *still* going to be *tremors,* and Deco City *isn't built* for this.

You need to protect the people in the meantime, okay?

Okay. Besides, it's *not* like we have a lot of other options.

That's the way it goes.

Love you, Hero Girl.

Love *you too,* Hero Boy.

THE TREMORS START...

Hallelujah! It *really does* rain men.

What?

The Weathergirls? 1982?

I guess I have to work on my *heroic banter.*

I guess so.

Everybody's a critic--*Wait,* do you *hear that?*

Hear *what?*

Oh, no!

The *bridge!*

RUMBLERUMBLERUM BLERUMBLERUMBLE

RUMBLERUMBLERUN BLERUMBLERUMBLE

ZOOM!

Hang on, **hang on!** I'm coming.

Okay, now--

Attention--

--everyone get off of the bridge! NOW!

Super *loud voice.*

Who would have known *that* was ever going to come in handy?

CRAKK!

Uh-oh...

Come on, stop *cracking!*

There are still *people* on--

Oh God, no.

THEN...

Crusader!

What's the *situation*, Amazonia? The city? How much *damage?*

You *stopped* the quakes. Property damage is *mostly minor*, and we're doing clean-up, but...

Mark, it's *Abby*--

ZOOM!

Sheesh! Let a girl finish a *sentence*, will you?

ABOVE DECO CITY...

Abby?

Abby, what's *wrong?*

⸮Sniff sniff!⸮

There was a tremor, Mark. And it hit the Vega Bridge. A section started to *collapse*.

Oh, *no.*

I *caught* it. I *stopped* it.

For a minute, at least. Then it *completely crumbled*.

Fifteen people fell off the bridge--

--and I could only catch *fourteen*.

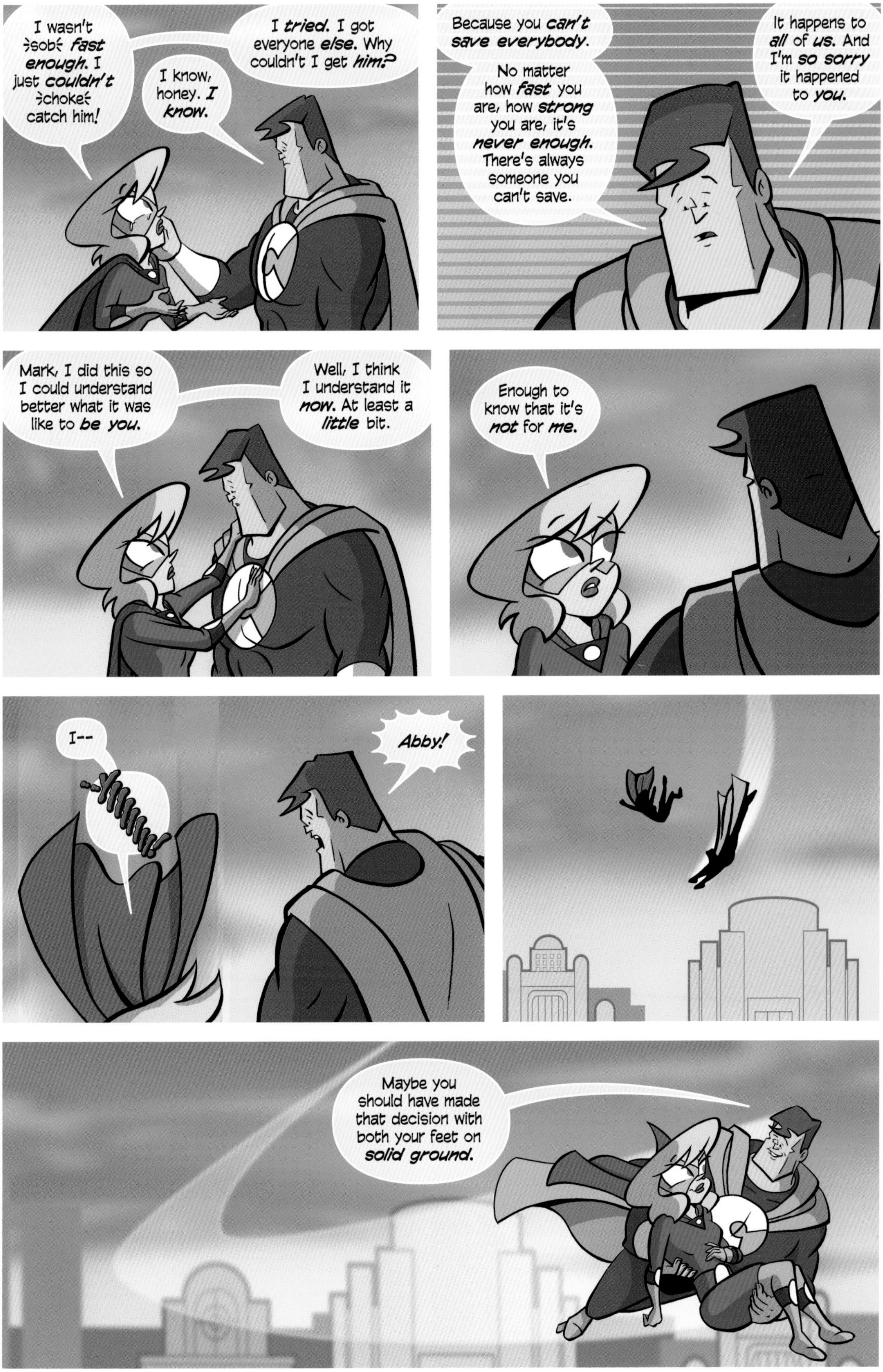

I wasn't ⊰sob⊱ *fast enough*. I just *couldn't* ⊰choke⊱ catch him!
I *tried*. I got everyone *else*. Why couldn't I get *him?*
I know, honey. *I know*.
Because you *can't save everybody*.
No matter how *fast* you are, how *strong* you are, it's *never enough*. There's always someone you can't save.
It happens to *all* of *us*. And I'm *so sorry* it happened to *you*.
Mark, I did this so I could understand better what it was like to *be you*.
Well, I think I understand it *now*. At least a *little* bit.
Enough to know that it's *not* for *me*.
I--
Abby!
Maybe you should have made that decision with both your feet on *solid ground*.

A FEW DAYS LATER...

No, we're *not* going out tonight. I'm just not feeling *up to it*.

I'm just going to *stay in* and read--

--hang *on* a minute, Charlotte.

Mark just showed up.

Mark, we're *not* going out--

Hey!

I'll take that.

Charlotte, it's Mark. *Sorry* to interrupt, but I think Abby needs some *cheering up.*

Oh, *thank God!* Any more of her moping and I was going to *Van Gogh* myself.

THE LIBERTY LEAGUE SATELLITE...

Mark, I *appreciate* you trying to help, but this is probably the *last* place I need to be right now.

Yeah, but *this* is also where *these* came.

You've got *mail.*

Mail?

Mark, what *is* all this?

They're *letters*, Abby.

From the people you *did* save.

108

Oh, my. There are *so many*.

Including a bunch of *kids' drawings?* Why would they--?

There was a *schoolbus* on that bridge, Abby. They *all* made it off because of you.

You'll *never know* exactly how many people you helped in your brief career.

See, that's the thing. While you'll *never* forget the person you *didn't* save--

--you can't forget all the people you *did*, either.

THEN...

Wait, so *why* can't I keep my letters?

Your apartment *isn't secure*, Abby. One *burglar* and *both* our secrets are out.

But we can store them *here*.

And *what* room is *this?*

It's our *storage area*. We heroes are surprisingly *sentimental* about our momentos.

It's kind of our *museum*.

Is that the *original* Golden Torch?

Yeah. She was never a *member* of the League, but helped us out a *few times*.

We like to remember our *friends*.

Especially the *cute* ones.

You did a *lot* of good, honey. You deserve a little bit of *recognition*. The *whole League* agreed.

Thank you.

Feeling *better* now?

Much.

And you know what? You were *right.* I *did* look kind of cute there.

You certainly wore your cape *well.*

END

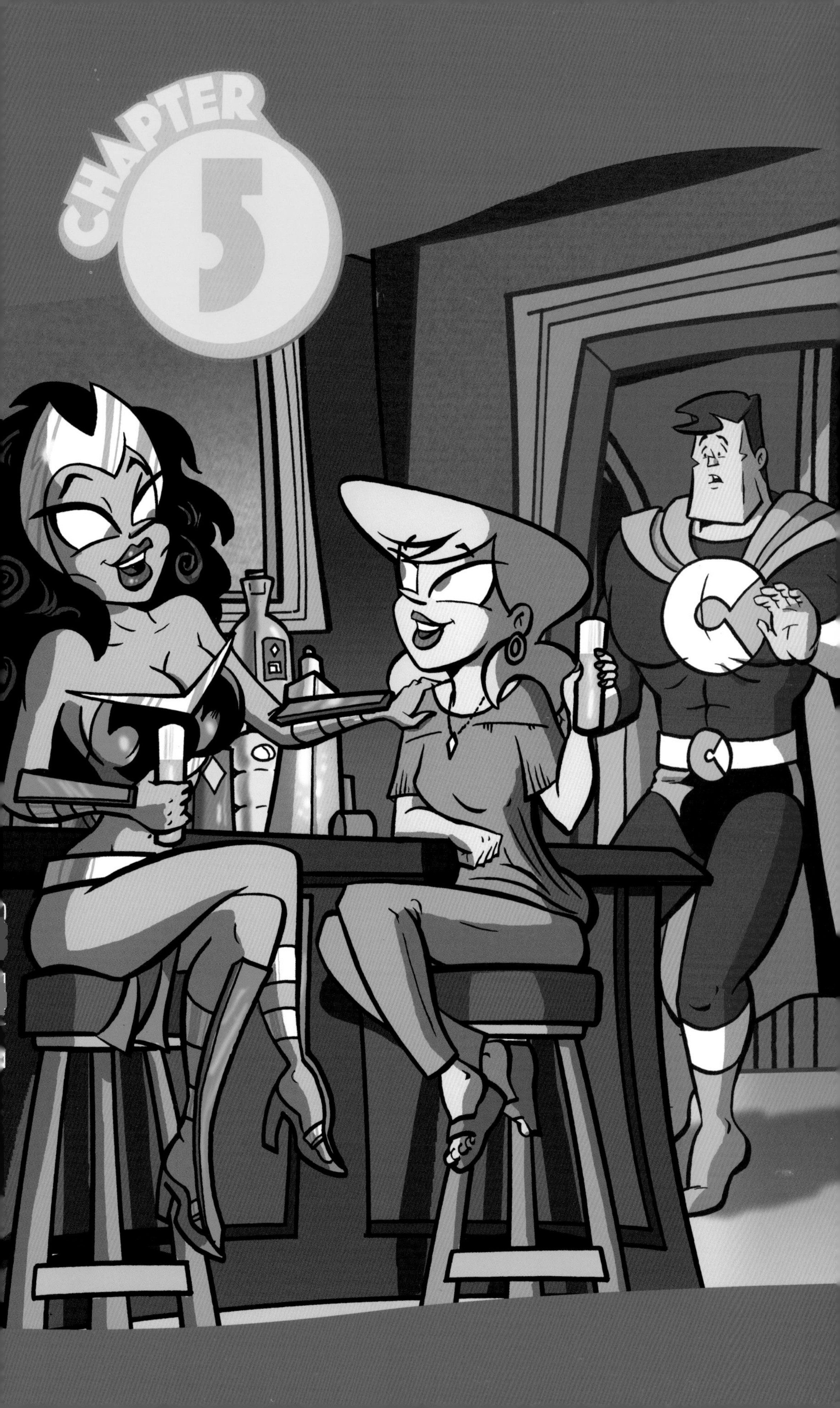
CHAPTER
5

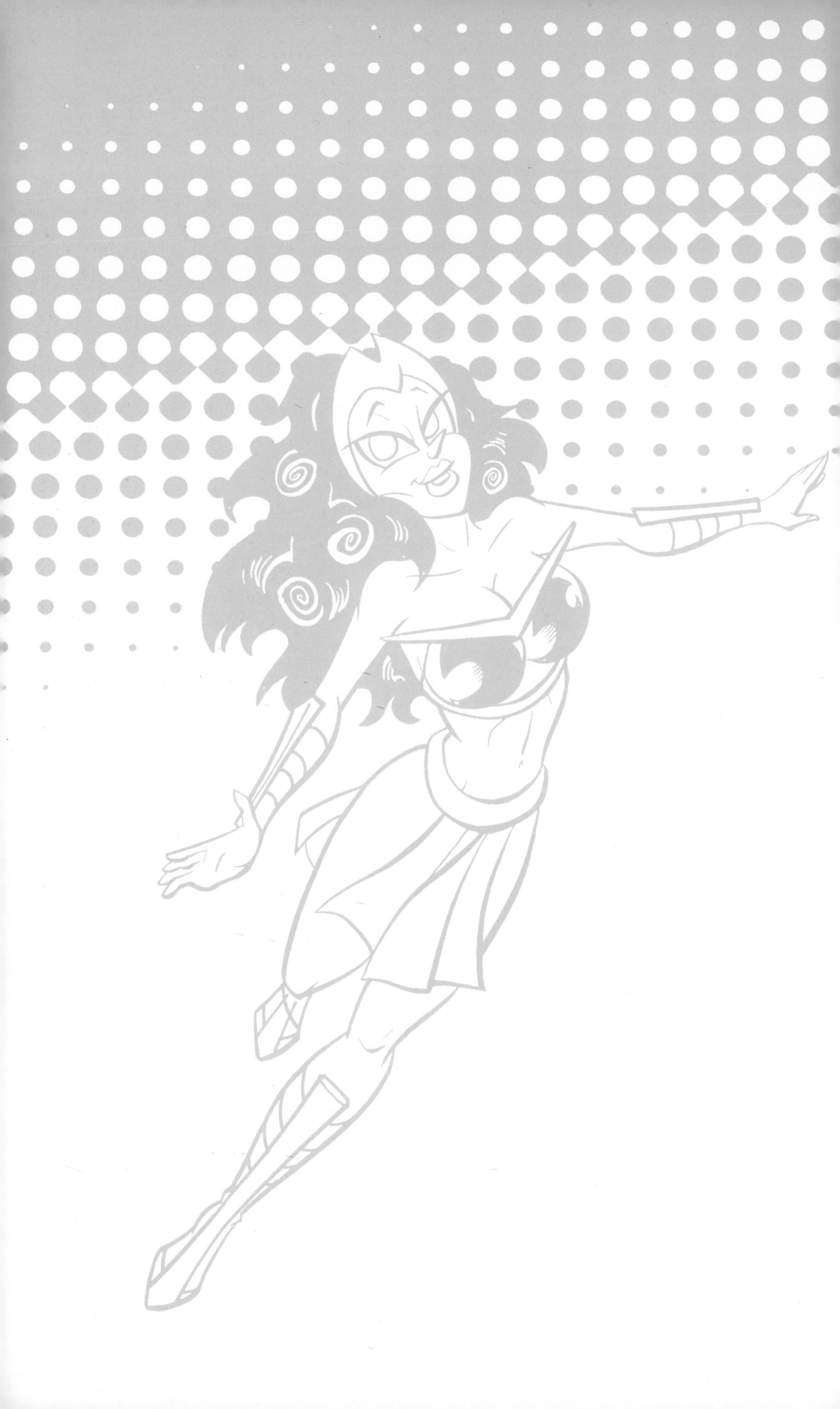

AT THE DECO VILLAGE MALL...

You mind if we stop in here for a minute, *Abby?* I still need to look at *tuxes.*

Sure, *Mark.*

Of course, if I don't find a wedding dress *soon,* you'll be standing on the altar in your tuxedo *alone.*

Thanks for planting *that* worry in my head.

Sorry. I just want *everything* to be *perfect,* and the right dress is a *huge* part of that.

I've been looking almost *non-stop* since you proposed, and I *still* can't find anything I like to--

Hey, I like *this* one! And with this *vest.* What do *you* think?

I think sometimes I *hate* being a girl.

THEN...

Mark, what's going to happen if I *can't* find a dress I like?

First, I don't want you to find one you *like,* I want you to find one you *love.*

And second?

I just want you to know I *get* it.

When I decided to become a super hero, I spent *weeks* designing uniforms, choosing colors and insignias and--

--um--

--it's still *nothing* compared to what you're going through. Don't even know *why* I brought it up.

Sorry.

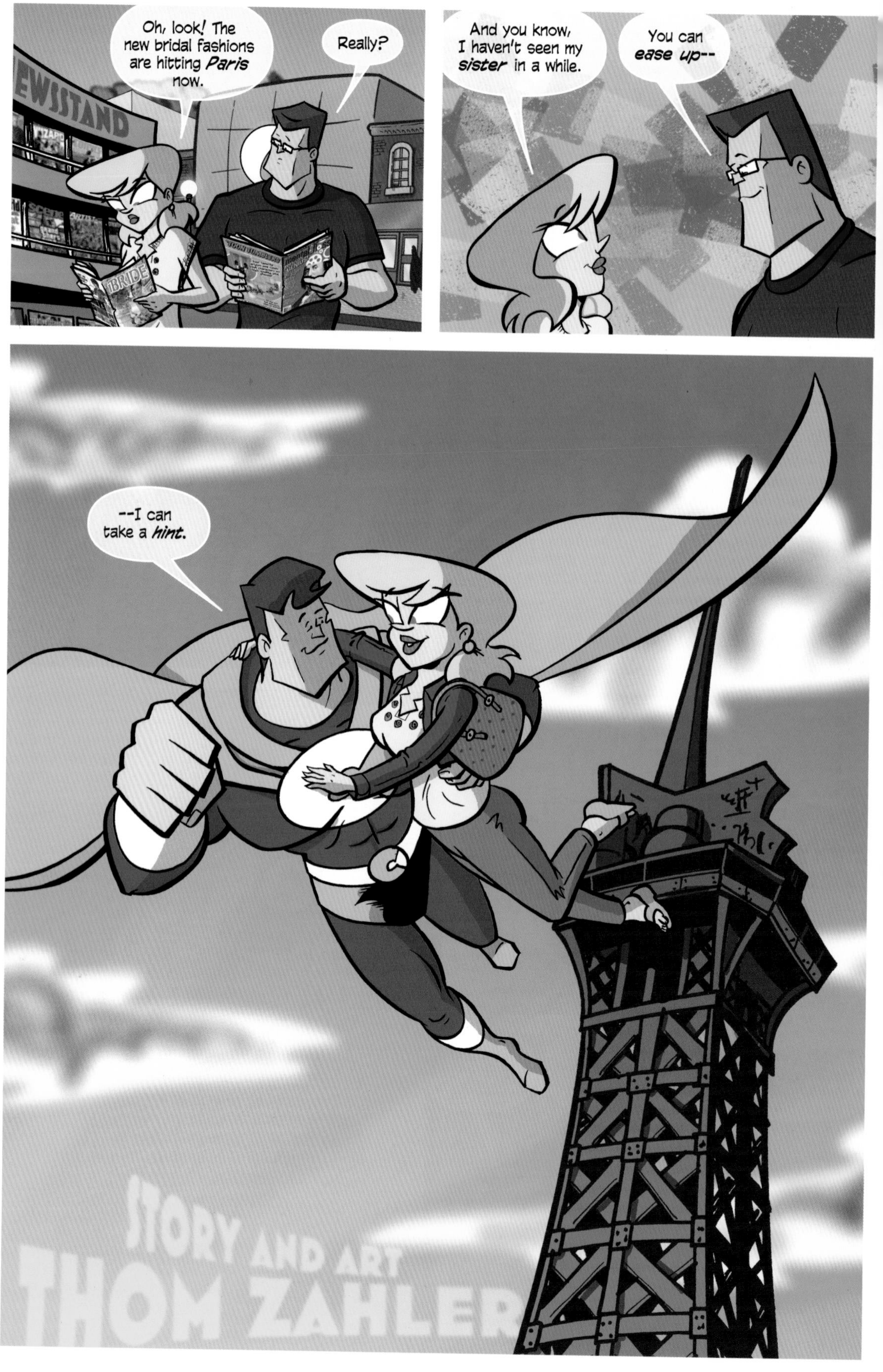
NEWSSTAND
Oh, look! The new bridal fashions are hitting *Paris* now.
BRIDE
Really?
And you know, I haven't seen my *sister* in a while.
You can *ease up*--
--I can take a *hint*.
STORY AND ART
THOM ZAHLER

SHORTLY...

So *what's* new in the world of *wedding* planning?

Well, I've started moving some of my stuff to *Mark's* apartment.

My *lease* expires next month, so I'll move back in with *Mom and Dad* until the wedding.

And then, when *his* expires in December, we'll find a *new* place.

Really? I always liked Mark's place. It's right there in *Presidents' Corner.*

Yes, but we need something a little more *couple-friendly.*

How so?

Bigger closets for one. Do you know how much space you lose to a *secret costume compartment?*

THEN...

Ma Journée Spéciale

Abby, can we stop for something to *eat* soon? This is kind of turning into the *Bataan Dress March.*

After *this* place, okay?

No... no... no.

Do you even *know* what you're looking for anymore?

Not really. But I'm sure I'll *know* it when I see it.

Did you look at the ones over *there?*

No, I--

Charlotte--

THAT'S THE ONE!

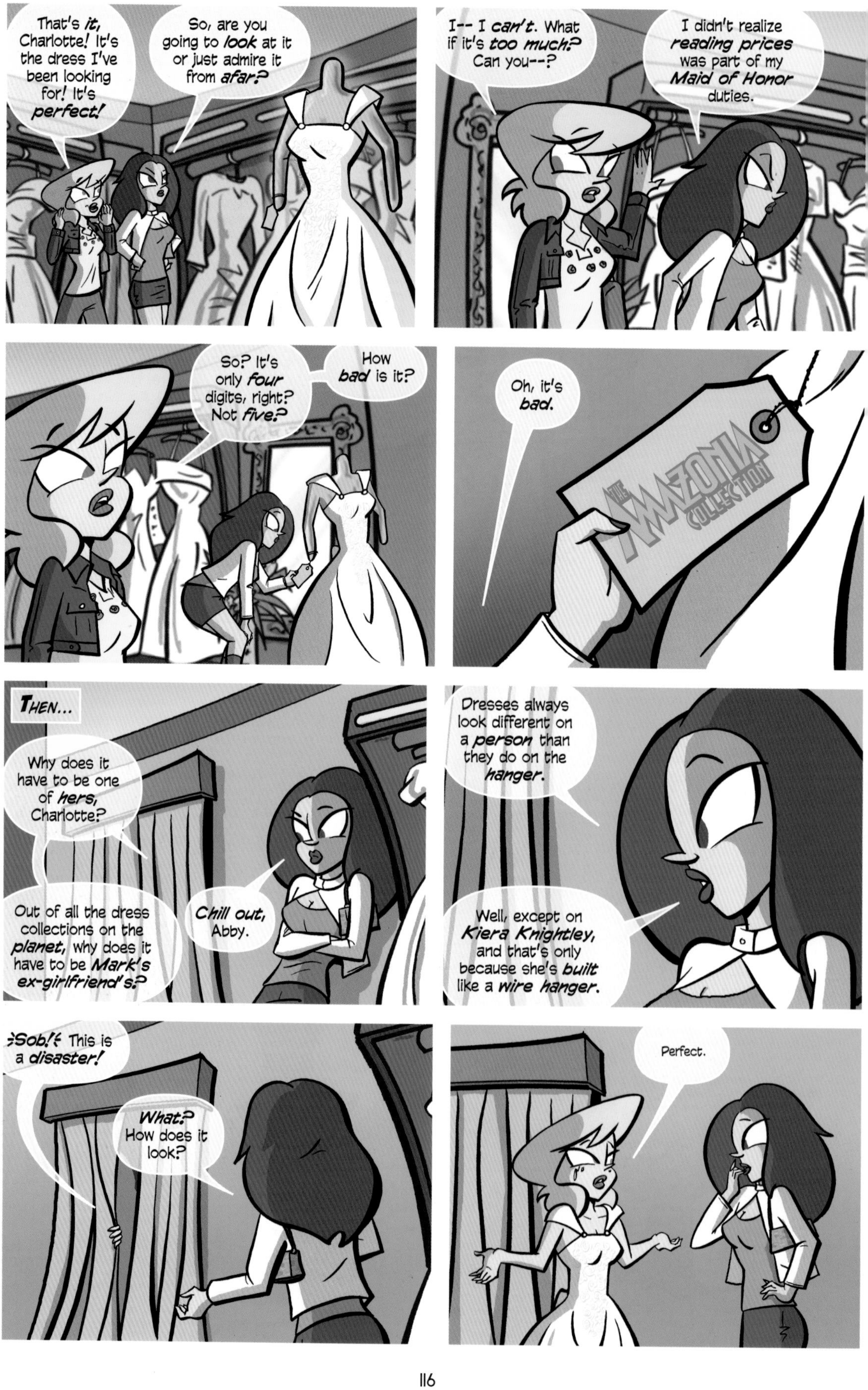
That's it, Charlotte! It's the dress I've been looking for! It's perfect!
So, are you going to look at it or just admire it from afar?
I-- I can't. What if it's too much? Can you--?
I didn't realize reading prices was part of my Maid of Honor duties.
How bad is it?
So? It's only four digits, right? Not five?
Oh, it's bad.
THE AMAZONIA COLLECTION
THEN...
Why does it have to be one of hers, Charlotte?
Out of all the dress collections on the planet, why does it have to be Mark's ex-girlfriend's?
Chill out, Abby.
Dresses always look different on a person than they do on the hanger.
Well, except on Kiera Knightley, and that's only because she's built like a wire hanger.
Sob! This is a disaster!
What? How does it look?
Perfect.

LATER...

Hi, Mark.

Hey, ladies. How did the *shopping* go?

Well...

What? What's with the *gloomy face?*

I found a dress that I *thought* was great, but then I looked at the *tag*.

Really? What did it *cost?*

Just her *soul.*

THEN...

Talk to you *soon*, Charlotte.

See you guys *later*. Have a safe trip back.

Yadda yadda yadda--

Okay, Mark, I *know* you can hear me. So *listen up.*

Abby did find a dress she *absolutely adored*. And she looked *perfect* in it.

The thing is, it's part of the *Amazonia collection*, which, in addition to the whole *ick factor*, also puts it north of the cost of *my car.*

So, I don't know *what* you're going to do about it, but you've got to figure out *something.*

You save the *day* all the time, right?. Now it's time to save your *wedding day.*

Hey, what's up? Now *you've* got the *gloomy face.*

Have to rush off to prevent some *crisis?*

Not right now--

--but I'll have to *address* it later.

So *how much* does one of her dresses-- *holy moley!* I've produced *films* for less.

I know, right? It's *crazy*. But Abby *really* loves it.

And *you* rescue so many people, how can you *not* try to save Abby on this?

Exactly.

So, I turn to my *exceedingly brilliant best friend* for advice.

You're in a *static system* right now. Nothing's moving. So you need to introduce some *entropy* into it.

You need to *tell Amazonia* and see what happens.

Oh, wait--you were expecting *me* to just buy the dress for you, weren't you?

Not *"expecting"* so much as *"hoping,"* really.

THE LIBERTY LEAGUE SATELLITE...

Don't forget, everyone, the next meeting is on the 16th.

Amazonia, could you *hold up* a minute?

Sure.

So, uh, Abby's been wedding dress shopping and she found one she *adores*.

It's one of *yours*.

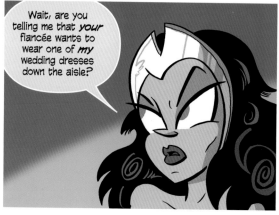

Wait, are you telling me that *your* fiancée wants to wear one of *my* wedding dresses down the aisle?

Um, yeah.

Well, this is *galactically awkward*.

Couldn't have said it better myself.

So Abby likes my dress line. You know, they're kind of *expensive*--

I noticed.

Hey, *I've* got an idea! Why don't you bring her to *my dimension*, and I'll have my royal dressmakers *custom make* her dress.

In fact, make a *weekend* of it. I'll take care of everything. It'll be *my wedding present* to the two of you.

Zoe, that's, um--

--wow--

--I'll have to talk with Abby about it, but *thank you.*

Watch her. I think she might be a *clone.*

I'm on it.

So...

Zoe, I couldn't help but *over-hear--*

That's because you were *lurking*, Paul.

Occupational hazard.

You're wondering why I made that *grand gesture* to Mark.

You have to admit, it's a little *out of character*, especially knowing what I know.

That's true.

But I have to accept that they're getting married no matter *how* I may feel. So I need to be a *better person* about this thing.

This is me trying.

You realize, of course, that this kindness is going to *confuse* Abby, too. Probably even cause her some *grief.*

I said I'm *trying* to be better--

--*not* that I'm *succeeding.*

THE NEXT MORNING...

This was a *great* idea, Mark. I haven't had these strawberry waffles in *forever*.

Good.

So, look, I talked to Charlotte and she *told me* about the wedding dress you saw in Paris--

What? She shouldn't have said *anything* about that!

Be *kind*. She was just trying to help.

For *now*, what would you say if I said I have a way for you to get that dress-- *custom made*--for you, for *free*?

I'd say "*What's the catch?*"

Yeah, there *is* a bit of a catch I guess.

We've been invited to go to *Leandia* as guests to get the dress, *courtesy* of the *designer*.

The designer--?

AMAZONIA!

You told *her* about this? How *could you?*

Abby, *please*, you're being a little *loud*.

Oh my God, *that's* why you brought me here, isn't it? So I wouldn't make a *scene?*

Was I *wrong?*

No. In fact, it's probably the *only* reason you're not *wearing* those pancakes right now.

Mark, do you *really* think I want a dress from Amazonia?

I realize it wouldn't be your *first* choice, no.

What are you doing? Calling for *backup?*

Actually, yes.

What?

Abby, do you think I *don't understand* how uncomfortable this is for you? I made sure to get *advice* on this.

Here. Someone wants to talk to you.

PARIS...

It's a *free* dress, you moron!

SHORTLY...

Charlotte, how could *you* let Mark think this was a *good idea?*

Because it *is.*

Because the only thing that lit up more than your *face* when you saw it was the *room* when you put that dress on.

Because that's The *Dress.*

Look at it this way: Amazonia's going to have to watch *her* dress get married to Mark *without* her in it.

Yeah, *but...* but...

No, wait, that actually clears *every-thing* up.

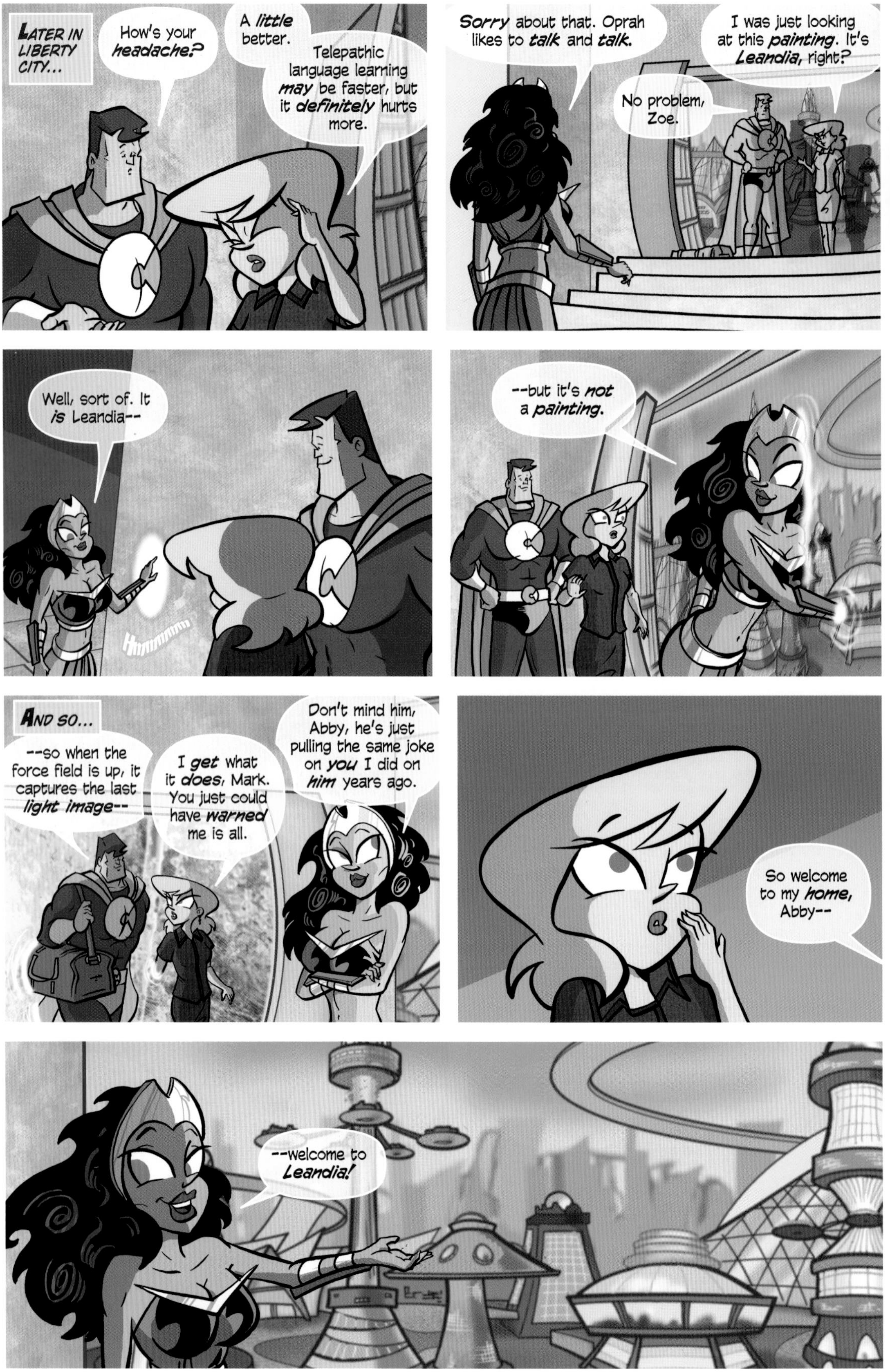
Later in Liberty City...
How's your headache?
A little better.
Telepathic language learning may be faster, but it definitely hurts more.
Sorry about that. Oprah likes to talk and talk.
I was just looking at this painting. It's Leandia, right?
No problem, Zoe.
Well, sort of. It is Leandia--
Hmmmmmm
--but it's not a painting.
And so...
--so when the force field is up, it captures the last light image--
I get what it does, Mark. You just could have warned me is all.
Don't mind him, Abby, he's just pulling the same joke on you I did on him years ago.
So welcome to my home, Abby--
--welcome to Leandia!

SHORTLY...

My mother's castle *isn't far* now.

If you look over there, you can see the *fire fountains* erupting.

And over there is the *Zhau Chan Academy* where I went to school--

So, what do you think *so far?*

It's a *gorgeous* place, Mark.

And the *people*--

Well, is there a law mandating a *maximum* of *three percent body fat?*

Yes, but don't worry, Zoe got us a *visa.*

CASTLE FORTIMUS...

All hail! Princess Amazonia has returned.

Zashi, Oriana! It's *good* to see you again.

Zashi, little sister! It's been *too long.*

Oriana, this is Abby. And you remember Mark, I'm sure.

Mark. *Of course.*

Come on. *Mother's* expecting us.

Say, Mark, is this going to be *weird* for you, being around your ex's family *all weekend?*

Just figuring that out *now,* are you?

Zashi. Mother.

Ah, the *Princess Amazonia* returns to these chambers!

Queen Mother, allow me to present *Abigail Tennyson* and *Mark Spencer*.

Zashi, Your Majesty.

I bid you *welcome* to my kingdom, Abigail. May your stay be *pleasant*.

And, of course, *Sir Mark* needs *no* introduction here.

Sir Mark?

Yeah, that's kind of a *long story*.

The House of Leandia is *always* pleased to have visitors.

I have arranged a *royal reception* for you tomorrow night.

Your Majesty, that's *very* kind--

--but you *don't* have to do that. *Really*.

Nonsense. You've made Leandia a part of your nuptuals, and we shall honor that.

Besides, *any* time the Princess *deigns* to return home is cause for *celebration.*

Mother! I was home for my birthday just *last month.*

Of course you were.

We had *presents.*

THEN...

If not, we can *surely* find--

We hope you will find these *diplomatic guest quarters* suitable.

These are *more* than fine. Please relay our gratitude to the Queen.

The Princess will send someone to *escort* you to your fitting *tomorrow morning*.

Do you require *anything else?*

No, I think we're *good.*

Thank you.

So these are their *diplomatic* quarters?

Yeah. It's kind of the Leandian equivalent of the *Lincoln Bedroom.*

Oh, *sure,* I can see that--

--if the White House was on the *Vegas* strip.

Does kind of have a *Caesar's Palace* vibe, *doesn't* it?

LATER...

All right, Mark, time to *come clean.*

How did you get yourself *knighted* here?

Oh, *that?*

Some *dragons* came through a dimensional rift. They were *frightened* and started *attacking* the city.

The Leandian army would have had to *kill* the poor guys. *I* managed to catch them all and send them *back home.*

So, the Queen *knighted* me.

I know it's just a title, but it's got to be *cool* to be Sir Mark. Too bad you were never knighted back on *Earth.*

Well... um, *actually*--

Oh my-- you *were* knighted back home, too, *weren't you?*

No, only *British citizens* can be knighted.

I'm, um, a *Commander of the Victorian Order.*

125

THE NEXT DAY...

Sorry to have to wake you up *so early*, Abby.

Don't worry. As long as I have *coffee*, I'll be fine.

I *am* surprised that Leandia has a *Starbucks* though.

Trade with your world goes *both ways*.

Now, there are a couple things I should probably *warn* you about.

First is that our *fitting process* is kind of *involved*.

There's a *reason* why I've been able to fight crime in *this* outfit for five years with *no wardrobe malfunctions*.

Well, I'd rather not have one of those at my wedding, so *that's* fine.

What's the *other* thing?

Well, I hope you *don't mind*, but--

--I invited a *friend*.

Surprise!

CHARLOTTE!

Amazonia, *why* did you-- *how*--?

It wouldn't be right for you to do this *without* your Maid of Honor, so I brought her through this morning.

Besides, *she'll* need a *bridesmaid dress*, too, right?

This is *okay*, isn't it?

This is *great*, thank you.

Abby, Charlotte, this is *Sura*.

She's been the *royal dressmaker* since I was a little girl. She even designed *my uniform*.

Pleased to meet you both. Now, let's *get started*.

Go ahead and take *off* your *clothes* and get in the *algae pit*.

Um, say that again?

126

LATER...

Abby and Charlotte shouldn't be *too much* longer, Mark.

Okay. *Thanks,* Zoe.

YOW!

Abby--?

Whoa, hey. *Don't worry,* everything's *fine.*

She just wasn't ready for the *ice.*

Ice?

FINALLY...

All *fitted,* Abby?

Abby?

How did it go? I heard--

I *don't* want to talk about it.

I hope the *dresses* are worth it, Mark. Heck, I hope *you're* worth it.

What?

Charlotte, *what happened* in there?

Hey-- are you *limping?*

THAT EVENING...

This is pretty *exciting*. A *royal reception*, in honor of *you two*.

Well, it *is* very nice of the Queen to do this.

So, if I meet a *prince*, I'm going to leave my *shoe* behind so he can search for me.

Abby? You're kind of *quiet*.

Or, I could just *tell him* how to find you.

Way to *ruin* the *fairy tale*, Mark.

I don't want to seem *ungrateful*, but I could do *without* all the attention.

I'll be happy if we *slip in* without too much of a *fuss*, stay a socially appropriate amount of time, and sneak out *unnoticed*.

PREDICTABLY...

HEAR YE, ALL--

"ANNOUNCING THE ARRIVAL OF SIR MARK, AND HIS BETHROTHED, ABIGAIL."

Oh, it's gonna be a *long* evening.

AND SO...

How went the *fitting*, Daughter?

Our *process* caught her a bit by surprise, but other than that it went well.

The dress she chose is *beautiful*, and Sura did some of her *finest* work, but--

--when Abby put on the dress, it became *transcendant*.

It was all *her*, Mother. Her love for him is *so great*, she made that dress *sing*.

Sometimes, I wonder if *I'll* ever have the chance to wear a *wedding dress* like *that*.

Oh, child--

--historically, *many women* in our family have remained *unwed*.

Thanks, mother. You always know *just* what to say.

THEN...

Attention, everyone. May I have your attention?

I'd like to make a *toast*--

--to our *guests of honor.*

Abigail, your radiant presence has brightened our fair kingdom. We are *pleased* to call you friend.

While *Sir Mark* we have known for *years*--

--and in all that time we have *never seen you happier.*

You two truly make a *perfect couple.*

Daughter, where are you going?

I need *another drink.*

Something a *lot* stronger.

CLAP! CLAP! CLAP!

LATER...

How does she *do* it? How does she just *walk in a room* and have guys just *gravitate* towards her.

Mark?

Wha--?

I said--

Mark, that's your "*I have to leave*" face. *Why* is that your "I have to leave" face?

Because I *have* to.

The *Celestial Hunger* has found Earth again. *Don't worry*, we can use the *Doosix Machine* to stop him.

Unfortunately, since *I* discovered the machine, it's *genetically locked* to *my* DNA and--

--and you've *stopped listening*, haven't you?

Yes. The *sooner* you *stop talking*, the sooner you *leave*, and the sooner you *get back.*

And the *less mad* I'll be when you *return.*

Consider the sound barrier *broken.*

Hey--!

Abby?

Who?

You're pretty *far* from the ballroom. *Hiding* from something?

Hiding? I'm not hiding. I'm just, ah, looking for a *restroom.*

Well, in that case you missed about *six* of them on your way down here.

Ooops.

You want to tell me *what happened* up there?

Oh, Mark got *called away.* I guess the *Celestial Hunger* showed up--

--and *he's* the only one who can run the Doosix Machine, *sure.*

Anyway, I hung out with Charlotte for a bit, but then she started *chatting up* a guy and I was the *third wheel.*

After *that,* I didn't see much of a reason to *stick around.*

So, Mark and Charlotte *abandoned* you, and now you've wound up in the *ambrosia cellar* with your fiancée's *ex-girlfriend.*

You're just having a *banner night,* aren't you?

That about *sums it up.*

Sorry to hear it.

Say, I'm going to grab *another bottle.* You want one?

Lord, I thought you'd *never* ask.

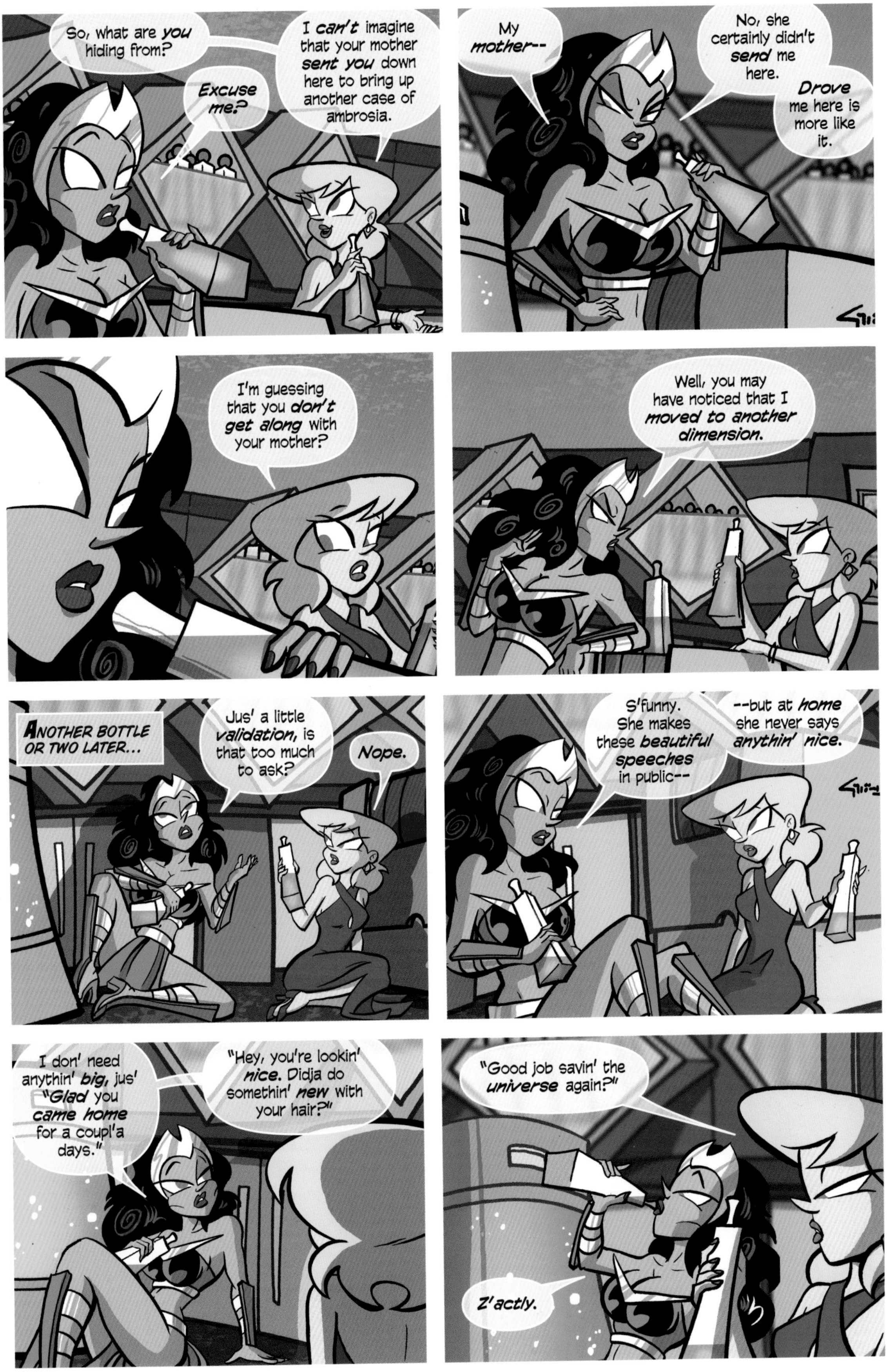
So, what are you hiding from?
Excuse me?
I can't imagine that your mother sent you down here to bring up another case of ambrosia.
My mother--
No, she certainly didn't send me here.
Drove me here is more like it.
I'm guessing that you don't get along with your mother?
Well, you may have noticed that I moved to another dimension.
ANOTHER BOTTLE OR TWO LATER...
Jus' a little validation, is that too much to ask?
Nope.
S'funny. She makes these beautiful speeches in public--
--but at home she never says anythin' nice.
I don' need anythin' big, jus' "Glad you came home for a coupl'a days."
"Hey, you're lookin' nice. Didja do somethin' new with your hair?"
"Good job savin' the universe again?"
Z'actly.

If it makes y'feel better, I've dealt with a *tough mom*, too.

Your mother is *diff'cult?*

Oh, no. My mom's *great*. We get along *jus' fine*.

I'm talkin' about one *Mrs. Joanne Spencer*.

Mark's mother. Oh yeah, I *forgot* 'bout her.

You didn't *forget*. You *blocked her out*. Like pos' traumatic stress.

Yeah, she was a *trip* all right. Still, I'd take her over *my* mother.

Really?

Joanne's a lotta things, but *shy* 'bout 'spressing her feelings *isn't* one of 'em.

Even so, *any* woman who is willing t'marry into Joanne's family is a *better woman'n* me.

'Bout *time* you realized that.

Y'know, when we first met, I got th' impression you *didn't* like me.

I wouldn't *say* that--

S'okay, I didn't like *you*, either.

I didn't like you because you an' Mark were jus' *so perfect*. I *knew* you'd get married 'ventually.

But he's still m'*friend*. An' you make him *happy*. So I hope you'll see the dress as a *peace offerin'*.

⧽Sigh!⧽ My dress...

I *LOVE* my dress.

It was *really nice*'a you. *Thank you, Zoe.*

All right, I'm feelin' good an' *validated*. You can *let go* now.

I *can't*. You're the only thing keepin' th' room from *spinnin'*.

AND THEN...

Charlotte, have you *seen* Abby, I--

Mark! Thank God you're here! *Something's* happened.

What? *What* happened, Charlotte?

Come on! You've *got* to see it for *yourself.*

--so he did that t'*you,* too?

Oh, sweet Lord.

All o'the time.

Hiya, Mark.

Hey, honey. Wanna drink?

No. I've got a feeling you've had enough for the *both* of us.

You ready to go *home?*

Yeah, m'ready.

Charlotte, would you mind *helping Abby* to our room? I'll take care of Zoe.

Are you sure that you don't want *me* to handle your ex?

If you think you can take care of the *drunk lady* who can *bench press* a *Buick,* be my guest.

You know, on second thought, maybe *I'll* handle Abby.

Good choice.

133

Don' worry 'bout *me*, Mark. I can stumble back t'my room by m'self. Take care of *your bride-t'be.*
Are you *sure?*
I'll be *fine.*
Y'know, tonight was actually kind'a *fun.*
It was great tradin' stories with Abby about *you.*
Me?
THE NEXT MORNING, BACK ON EARTH...
Good morning, honey. I was just checking to see how the *morning after* was treating you.
Not *too* badly, all things considered. A slight *headache*. And last night's a bit *blurry*. I hope I didn't do anything stupid.
Just your *female bonding* with Amazonia.
Yeah, that was-- *interesting,* wasn't it? It was probably the first time I've *really talked* to her.
We're *never* going to be *friends,* but I think we'll at least be more *friendly.*
Friendly enough to invite her to the *wedding?*
Don't mistake this *détente* for an *armistice*.
Really? Beacause I hear the *best* relationships are the ones you can talk about in *military terms.*

Good morning, *Jason.*

Hey, look who's *back!*

So, what did I *miss?*

Not *too* much. Normal traffic for a weekend.

Oh, and they announced a street date for the new *Rick Castle* book, so I started taking orders for it.

Excellent. I do have a wedding to pay for, you know.

You've mentioned it *once* or *twice.*

So, how was the cabin in *Canada?*

Well--

--it was like a *completely different world.*

Anything *else* new?

There was a *message* on the *voice mail* this morning. I didn't get a chance to pull it, though.

It's probably just *Mark's mom.* She's got my cell and work numbers mixed up in her phone.

They're coming in next weekend to meet *my parents* for the *first time* and--

--what's *that* look for?

It's just... that's the *first time* I've heard you mention your future mother-in-law and *not* get that *vomit face* expression.

I guess I must be *mellowing.* She just doesn't seem like quite the *royal pain* I used to think she was.

Heh. Vomit face. That was pretty good.

135

Please enter your *passcode*.

BEEP! BEEP!

You have *one* message.

Hi, Abby, it's *Zoe*. Sorry to call you at work, but it's the *only number* I had for you.

Look, I just wanted to say that last night meant *a lot* to me. It was good to *actually talk* to you.

I know our relationship is, well, *complicated*. So I appreciate the effort--

--and I *especially* appreciate you *inviting me to your wedding*.

THEN...

Hey, honey. Guess who invited your ex-girlfriend to our wedding while on her *bacchanal* last night?

Hmmm, I'm *not sure*. Maybe I should give *Darkblade* a call.

So *what* are you going to do?

Well, I can't really *disinvite* her now, can I?

I guess.

I suppose not. You know, *don't worry* about it. It'll be *fine*.

AND SO...

Hey, did you get the *message?*

Oh, yeah. I *got it* all right--

--and I will *never* drink *that* much again.

END

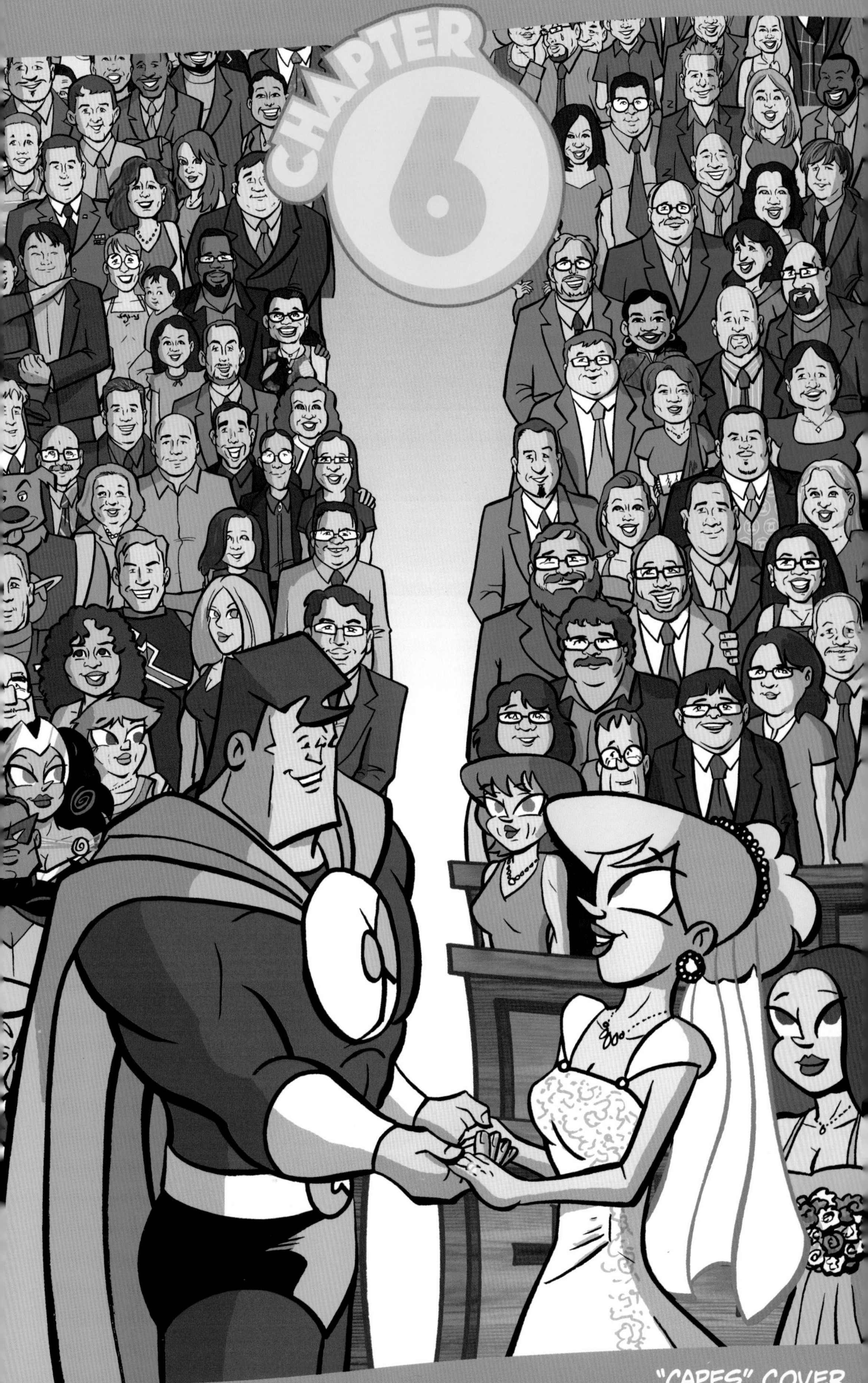
CHAPTER
6

"CAPES" COVER

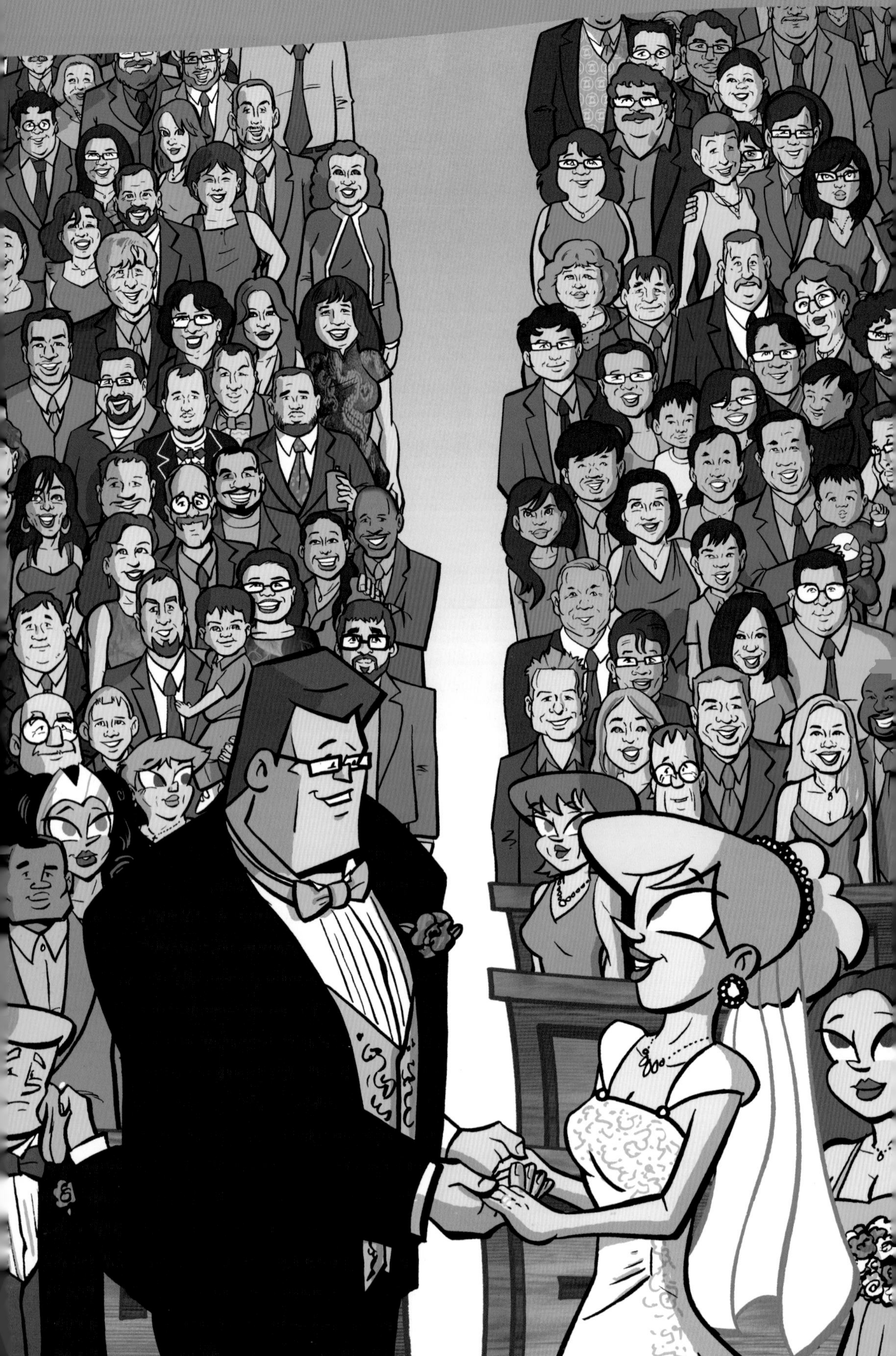

"LOVE" COVE

THE NIGHT BEFORE THE WEDDING...

All right, ladies, I'm heading to *bed*.

Good night, *Dad*.

Thanks again, Dad. It was a *wonderful toast*.

I think Dad has the *right idea*, Mom. I should probably get to bed, too.

Just a little bit longer, Abby. Tonight's the *last night* I get to enjoy having *both* my daughters under my *roof*.

It's been *so nice* having you back home.

And it's been nice *being back*, Mom.

But *don't worry*. Even after *I'm* married--

--you'll *still* have Charlotte.

So, found someone *else* to hold your dress when you're in the bathroom have you?

LATER...

You know, I *did* almost move out a *few years* back.

Yeah, but moving in with *me* doesn't count.

Too bad. I would have been a *great* roommate.

No offense, but I kind of *prefer* the one I found.

Hope you can manage to get *some* sleep tonight.

I'll be *fine*. Everything's taken care of.

--I *did* call the florist, right?

Oh, God. What about the *organist?*

Tap! Tap! Tap!

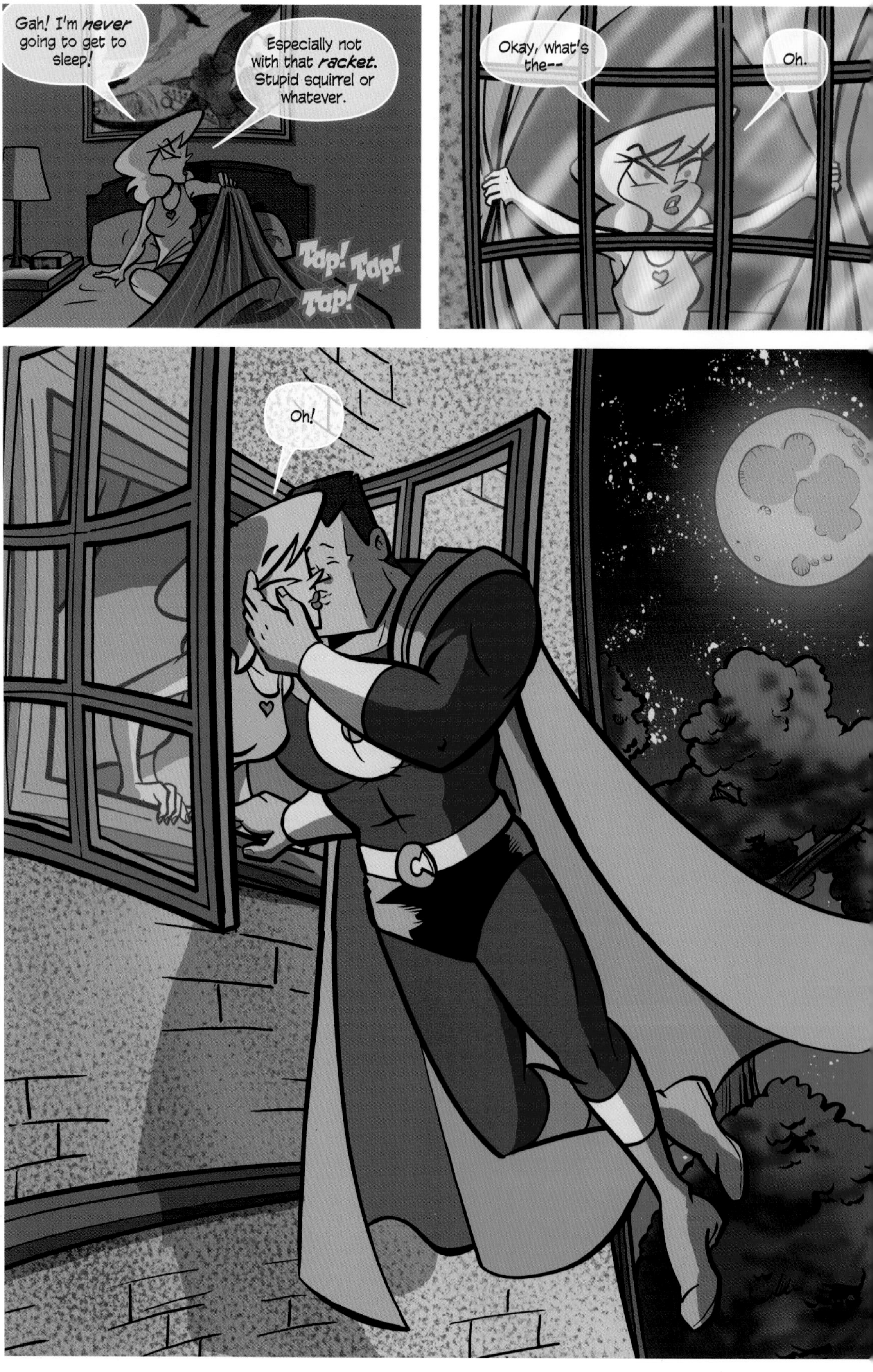
Gah! I'm *never* going to get to sleep!
Especially not with that *racket.* Stupid squirrel or whatever.
Tap! Tap! Tap!
Okay, what's the--
Oh.
Oh!

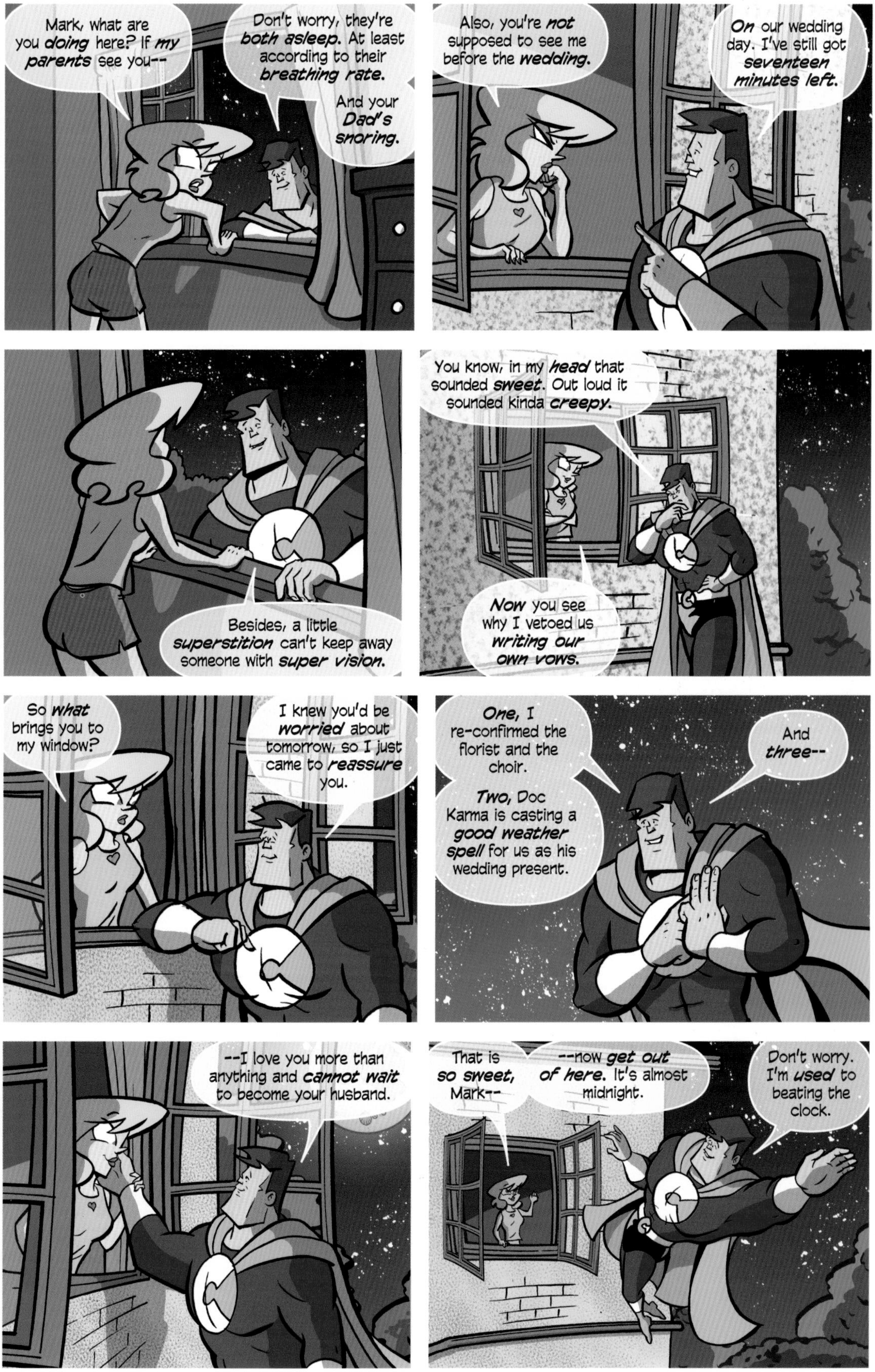

Mark, what are you doing here? If my parents see you--
Don't worry, they're both asleep. At least according to their breathing rate.
And your Dad's snoring.
Also, you're not supposed to see me before the wedding.
On our wedding day. I've still got seventeen minutes left.
Besides, a little superstition can't keep away someone with super vision.
You know, in my head that sounded sweet. Out loud it sounded kinda creepy.
Now you see why I vetoed us writing our own vows.
So what brings you to my window?
I knew you'd be worried about tomorrow, so I just came to reassure you.
One, I re-confirmed the florist and the choir.
Two, Doc Karma is casting a good weather spell for us as his wedding present.
And three--
--I love you more than anything and cannot wait to become your husband.
That is so sweet, Mark--
--now get out of here. It's almost midnight.
Don't worry. I'm used to beating the clock.

AND SO...

‡Sigh!‡

Why is it raining? I was promised *no* rain.

Why--

--why am I in my apartment?

Okay, guys, *very funny*. Mess with the bride on her wedding day.

I don't know how you got my *landlord* to let you back in--

--or *why* you went to the trouble of putting back *all* my stuff--

--but the joke's *over*.

What's going on here?

Well, for *one* thing, you're *waking up* your *roommate*.

Roommate?

Oh, that's right, you prefer *"freeloader."*

Now, what's got you so *riled up?*

This *stupid joke.* It's gone too far.

What stupid joke?

This one! Grabbing me from Mom and Dad's place. Setting my whole apartment back up.

What do you guys think you're doing?

I'm supposed to be *getting married today!*

Married? Abby, you haven't had a date since before I moved in here.

Not that I haven't tried, of course. But *noooo*--

--you're *too good* for anyone who's spent *any* time in prison.

This *can't* be happening.

Are you *serious?* Do you really *not* remember Mark?

And *Mark* is your imaginary fiancé?

You know, this was cute when you were *seven* and wanted to marry *Prince Eric.* Now it's just sad.

So is this Mark a prince, *too?*

No, he's the *Crusader.*

Now I *know* he's imaginary.

Why do you say *that?*

Because the Crusader died like *three years ago.*

What?

‡Sob!‡ I **don't understand.** Nothing makes **any** sense.

Abby, I think something's **really** wrong.

Maybe you should...**see** someone?

Who? **Paul?** Would he even--

I don't know **who** Paul is. I was thinking more of a **doctor.**

A **doctor?** Charlotte, you're a **genius.** That's **exactly** who I need to see!

Really? I figured you'd fight--

I need to go get **dressed.**

Um, just checking... **Doc Karma** is still alive, right?

‡Sigh!‡

DOCTOR CARMODY'S OFFICE...

I don't understand **how** this could have happened.

Everything's different.

10:17am

http://www.decocitytimesonline.biz

DECO CITY TIMES ONLINE

Crusade's End
A Hero Dies

A spokesman for the Liberty League announced today the Crusader was killed sometime last Friday, bringing an end to questions about the whereabouts of Deco City's resident superhero.

While no details of the Crusader's demise were released, several sources claim that the Evil Brain may be responsible.

Ms. Tennyson, **Dr. Carmody** will see you now.

Great. Thanks.

THEN...

Hello, Ms. Tennyson, I'm Doc--

Doc Karma! Thank God!

Um. ‡Cough cough!‡ **Excuse me?**

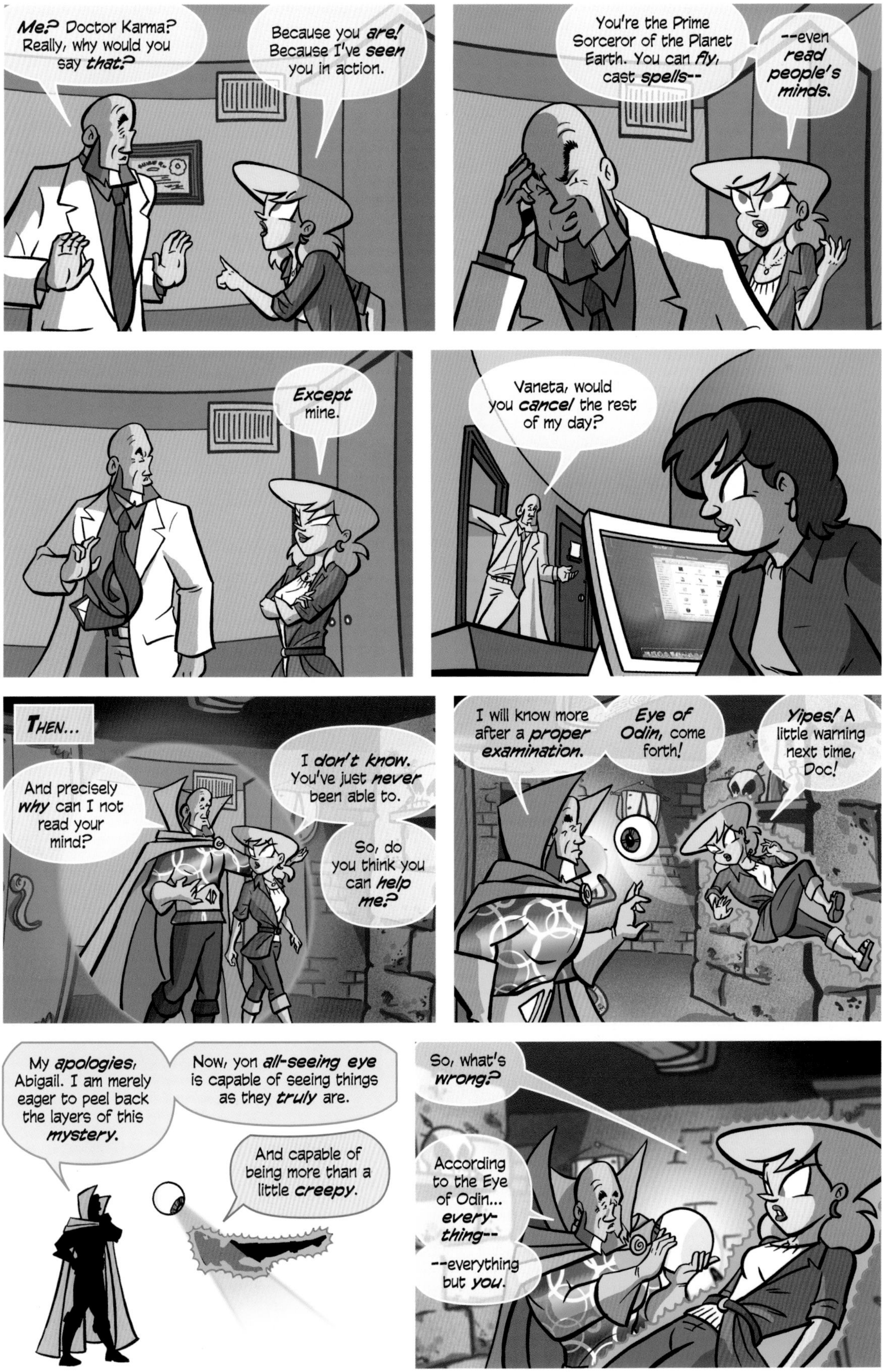

Me? Doctor Karma? Really, why would you say *that?*
Because you *are!* Because I've *seen* you in action.
You're the Prime Sorceror of the Planet Earth. You can *fly*, cast *spells*--
--even *read people's minds.*
Except mine.
Vaneta, would you *cancel* the rest of my day?
THEN...
And precisely *why* can I not read your mind?
I *don't know.* You've just *never* been able to.
So, do you think you can *help me?*
I will know more after a *proper examination.*
Eye of Odin, come forth!
Yipes! A little warning next time, Doc!
My *apologies*, Abigail. I am merely eager to peel back the layers of this *mystery.*
Now, yon *all-seeing eye* is capable of seeing things as they *truly* are.
And capable of being more than a little *creepy.*
So, what's *wrong?*
According to the Eye of Odin... *every-thing--*
--everything but *you.*

THE LIBERTY LEAGUE SATELLITE...

--and so I brought her *here*. I know you're *no longer* a member of the League, Darkblade, but I thought--

You did the *right thing*, Doctor.

Please continue.

As best as I can determine, the Evil Brain traveled *back* in time three years and, armed with his *foreknowledge*, was somehow able to complete his *sinister goal*.

It explains *everything*.

The Evil Brain always took *credit* for Mark's death, but *never* revealed *how*. An egotist like him would have relished revealing *every detail* to us--

--unless doing so could have *undone* his victory.

Now that we know *he* changed history to do it, *we* can change it *back*.

This *I* swear!

Still has quite the flair for the *dramatic*, doesn't he?

Just a little.

Doctor, make your preparations to send me back--

As is so often the case, our task is *not so simple*.

The time period in question seems to be *shielded*.

He must have built a *Time Knot*. It'd also explain how he avoided the *paradox issue*.

Aye, such a device *could* be responsible.

But, while I have discerned that no one from *our* timeline can pierce the accursed veil, I can send someone back from the *original* timeline.

Her? You want to trust Mark's life to a...*civilian?*

My friend, in the *unadulterated timeline*--

--Mark trusts her with *far more* than just his *life*.

146

It's *Annie*, right?

Abby.

Sorry. We're still working on a solution, Abby. I just had to *get out of there* for a minute.

Temporal mechanics always give me a *headache*.

So, in *your* timeline, you're *engaged* to Mark?

Yes.

And I'm *still alive?*

Yes.

Wow, I must be a real *bitch* to you there.

You know, you're *nothing* like the Amazonia from my world.

Oh, we're probably *more alike* than you think. Just *different circumstances.*

I know how I was after Mark and I broke up. I *always* thought we'd get back together.

I can *only imagine* what I'd be like if he started dating some *cute little blonde thing.* I'll bet I take *cattiness* to the level of *super power.*

Fortunately, you've got your *inner super strength* to handle your Amazonia, right?

Super strength? I'm *just* a normal girl.

Normal? Abby, you woke up in a situation that would send most people to an *institution*, and instead you're here helping to *change the universe.*

Wow, you're right.

I *rock.*

That's what I'm saying.

LATER...

All right, I went home and got a *cold weather clothes*. Care to tell me why?

Because Deco City has *bitter winters*.

We're going to send you *back in time* to the day Mark was killed. *March 15th*, three years ago.

His communicator stopped transmitting at *11:58pm local time*. You'll have until *then*.

If you cannot discern the *cause* of his demise, you will have to *warn him* and hope, like the proverbial *butterfly*, your minor action will have a *major effect*.

As for *finding* him, Mark liked a coffee shop on Kennedy Stree--

He'll be at Chez Ferrer at 8:30.

And just *how* do you know that so *precisely?*

I was with him. On *our first date*.

Say, with Abby running around a time and place she *already* exists--

--should we get her a *disguise?*

Good idea. I didn't think of that.

I did. Doctor--?

I have enchanted yon bauble with a *spell of deception*, so that whosoever wears it shall have their identity *shrouded*.

Just put it on?

Aye. 'Tis all.

So? Can you recognize me?

That's not really fair. It's not like we recognized you *before*, did we?

148

I must now summon the *Lady of the Flame* to send you back.

Indeed?

The Lady of the Flame? I *met her* once.

The Lady is a creature of *time*, Abigail. Just as we move ever *forward*, she moves *back*. 'Tis why I am asking her to take you on your *journey*.

It is surely within her power to *protect* you from the *ravages* of history's revision. *Even* to hide your thoughts from *me*.

But as to *why* I cannot say. For in planes *ethereal* or worlds *corporeal* there is one *constant mystery*--

--*women*.

Excuse me. The Lady is trying to make contact.

I'll *bet* she is.

AND...

You look *worried*, Abby.

Aren't *you?* I mean, if I succeed, you'll never *exist*, will you? Not *this* you, at least.

That's *true*, Abby. But *any* one of us here would sacrifice ourselves to bring Mark back.

Besides, we'll all *still be around*. Just a little *different*. And, as for *your* Amazonia, I'm sure she'll *move on* in time. Just as *I* have.

Abigail--

--'tis time--

--to step into the *fire*.

149

May the *fates* guide you in your quest, Abigail.

Good luck, Abby.

Bring him *back.*

So how does this *work,* Doc? Do I click my *heels* together or--

I'll do my *best.*

--*YIKES!*

FWOOOSH

DECO CITY...

THREE YEARS AGO...

FWOOOSH

Well, that was... *unpleasant.*

Still, I've got all my *clothes,* so it's better than *Terminator.*

All right, Bookstore Girl.

Time to *save the hero.*

MEANWHILE...

The sun is shining.

But the ice is slippery.

Greetings, *Evil Brain* from the future.

You know, when I created those *protocols* for making contact with my *past self*, I never thought I'd need them.

Just a testament to your *brilliance*, my past self.

As well as your *luck*. How did you steal *that* body while I got this *granola-crunching health nut?*

Why, when I possessed him, he was *jogging*. *Today*. In *this* weather!

Can you-- oh!

Your large *cheesy onion bacon loaf*, sir.

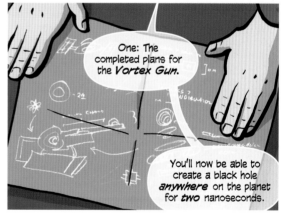

I *really* hate joggers.

Can I *assume* you didn't break the *time barrier* just to *ruin waist-lines?*

Quite right. I come bearing *two* presents.

One: The completed plans for the *Vortex Gun.*

You'll now be able to create a black hole *anywhere* on the planet for *two* nanoseconds.

I've been working on this for *weeks!* How did you-- An infindibulator? *Really?*

Curses! I really should have figured that out.

Don't be so hard on yourself. Given another *six months*, you would have.

The Vortex Gun is good for only *one* shot, though, and requires *twenty minutes* of prep time.

You would have to know the *precise* location of the Crusader ahead of time.

And I *do.*

Tonight, at 11:56pm, North Korea will conduct a missile test that will go *awry.* The Crusader will stick his nose into the matter and *intercept the missile.*

The thing that required three years' time was acquiring *this:*

The *telemetry from that missile.*

Giving us the Crusader's precise location. *Brilliant.*

So *how* did you acquire it? I can't imagine *Dear Leader* gave it up easily.

No, but Dear Leader never learned *not* to bet on an *inside straight,* either.

Then thank you for this, Future Evil Brain. I will get this data to my *actual* body.

And I'll *release* this one. You know how to contact me if you need.

Urk!

What? Where am I? How did I get here? What—

Good God, *what* did I eat?

RUMBLE! GURGLE!

ELSEWHERE...

"Mark, I'm from the *future*--"

Nah. Maybe "*Doc Karma* sent me?"

Heck with it, I'll just *improvise.*

MARK SPENCER C.P.A.

CLOSED FOR THE DAY DUE TO EMERGENCY (SORRY!)

What--?

M_SPENCER C.P.A.

CLOSED FOR THE DAY DUE TO EMERGEN (SORRY!)

Geez, Mark, you want to meet me *halfway* on this?

I've traveled through time *and* it's tax season. Why aren't you *here?*

MEANWHILE, IN CHRONOPOLIS...

Hit him kind of *hard,* didn't you?

Ah, he's *invulnerable.* He'll be fine.

Besides, I'm in a *hurry.* I've got a *date* tonight, you know.

MARK SPENCER C.P.A.

CLOSED FOR THE DAY DUE TO EMERGENCY (SORRY!)

Hmm, maybe I'm *overthinking* this. I *could* just call him.

He usually *forwards* his phone to his League communicator.

⸮Harrumph!�771; That's what I get for being an *early adopter,* I guess.

Time to find a *pay phone.*

SHORTLY...

⸮Sigh!�771; I remember when there *used* to be pay phones.

I should take a *moment,* collect my thoughts. Maybe get a--

K'S VID

GIDDY'S BOOKS AND COF

GIDDY'S BOOKS CO

--cup of coffee?

153

Oh, Abby, you *shouldn't* do this...you *shouldn't* do th--

≳Sigh!≳ Who are you kidding? How do you *not* do this?

Hello! Welcome to Abby's Books and Coffee.

What can we *help* you with?

Um, hi.

Ah, could I get a *triple-mocha almond caffeine-achino?*

Sure, coming right up!

DEATH OF A PROM QUEEN
Richard Castle

That's a really *nice coat*, by the way. I have one *just like it.*

Great minds think *alike*, I guess.

Thanks.

Feel free to take a *look around*, too. You never know when some *book* will catch your eye.

Abby, it's almost *three.* Don't you have a hair appointment today?

I've still got a *few* minutes before I have to leave and get all pretty for my *date*.

I *still* can't believe you're going out with your *accountant*. He's *so* not your type.

I don't know if you've noticed from my string of *truncated relationships*, but my "type" hasn't exactly been *good* to me.

Mark's a *nice guy*, and cute... in an *understated* sort of way.

So, why *shouldn't* I go out with him?

Oh, you've completely *given up*. Why didn't you just *say so?*

Okay, this is just *surreal.*

154

SHORTLY...

You have a *good time* on your date tonight with Mr. Excitement.

Geez, Charlotte, *lighten up.* It'll be fine.

So you don't need your standard *rescue call* half an hour into it this time?

No, I should be good.

I'm *sure* you will. If you run out of stuff to talk about, there's always--

--well, you said he loved that *Battlestar Galactica* show, right?

Um, on second thought, why *don't* you make that call tonight? Just to be *safe.*

THEN...

Darn it!

Something *wrong?*

Yeah, my *sitter* just called. My *newborn's* acting up, and the only thing that calms him down is when I *sing* to him--

--but my *phone just died.*

Tell you what, why don't I let you use the phone in the *back?* I used to babysit, and I know how bad those fits can be.

There's no problem with me going in your store-room?

Nah, I let people back here *all the time.*

I *knew*--

--knew you'd be cool about this.

155

C'mon... *c'mon...*

Hi, you've reached Mark Spencer's *voice mail.* Leave a message after the beep.

Beep!

Mark! Mark, thank God, it's--

--well, it's *not* important who I am.

But it *is* important that I know who *you are.*

And you are in a *lot of danger!*

You need to *watch yourself.* I can't tell you *how* it's going to happen, but you're *going to be killed today.*

Beep! Your message has been sent.

Wait! *What?*

Crap. I think I just threatened the Crusader.

Okay, Mark, I'm trying this again. I was sent *back* from the *future* by Doctor Karma to warn you that the Evil Brain is going to try to *kill you.*

We *don't know how,* but you've got to be *extra-*careful today. Especially tonight around *midnight.* That's all we know.

Okay, Lady of the Flame. I've *warned* him. So history's fixed now, *right?*

I'm ready to *go home* and get married now.

Did you get your baby calmed down?

No. Apparently, he's not *checking his messages* today.

156

THAT NIGHT...

May I take your **coats?**

Yes, please.

This way.

So, how are you both tonight?

Lovely, thank you.

You look **very nice** tonight, by the way.

I **really** like that dress.

Thank you, Mark..

Of **course** you liked it. I was **tarting it up** for you.

This was a **great choice,** Mark. I've always wanted to come here.

I'm **glad** you like it, Abby.

So, did you do anything **interesting** today?

Back to the **Cretaceous** with you, buddy!

No, not really.

157

This is going to be *painful*.

So, is that like an *ex-boyfriend* or something?

Wha--?

That couple you've been *staring* at?

Um, no. No, it's just some couple on a *first date*. But I *can't stop* watching them.

So *how's* he doing?

He's in a *nosedive*, but he doesn't realize it.

Why? Does he keep staring at her *chest* or something?

No, he's just not telling the *truth*.

--nah, I'm not really a big *flyer*. I like to stick close to home.

AND SO...

All right, Abby, there's something I've wanted to ask you for a *while*.

Well, it might be *inappropriate*, so saying *"no"* is a fine answer.

Go ahead.

Ah, will you be getting any *advance copies* of the new *Wally Wizarder* book?

What, do you have a *niece* or *nephew* who's really into it?

No, it's for *me*. I'm a *huge fan*.

Seriously? You're not just trying to *impress* a bookstore owner, are you?

I've been *trying like hell* to impress a bookstore owner all night.

But not with *that*.

So, you read *Wally Wizarder?*

I read a *lot* of things, but yeah, I'm a big fan of the Wally books.

Okay, Mark, let's hear it. What *else* do you read?

I feel like I'm being *tested*.

You *are*. But no pressure.

Anything really. Fiction, histories, biographies... *whatever*.

My job takes up a *lot of time*, and reading's one of the few things I can do at my *own pace*.

But, if you're putting me on the spot and asking for *authors*, I'd say Updike, Faulkner, McCarthy, Ellison...Twain and Steinbeck if you go classical. And, of course, Shakespeare.

So, how'd I do?

I have to say, I'm a little bit *turned on*. So I think you did fine.

You know, I opened up my bookstore *mostly* to support my book buying habit.

I've seen your *balance sheet*, Abby. I didn't really think you got into it for the *money*.

Very funny.

I started reading *before* kindergarten. Books have just *always* been part of my life.

So, what's on *your* nightstand?

Right now, I'm in the middle of the new *Nick Hornby* book.

What's *wrong?* Not a fan?

No, it's just-- your phone is *vibrating*.

You could hear it from *there?*

Well, I've got *pretty good* hearing.

Boooooop! This is the *Emergency Date Rescue Service*. If this is an *actual* emergency--

Sorry, you have the wrong number.

Click!

Guess it's *not*.

Sorry, that was--

A *fake emergency call* just in case the date went *south?*

Um... ah...

Busted, huh?

So, will *you* be getting one tonight, too?

No--

--if I get a call tonight, it *really will be* the end of the world.

All right, I'm going to *freshen up* and then we can go.

Okay. I'll get the *check*.

Mark--

--we need to talk.

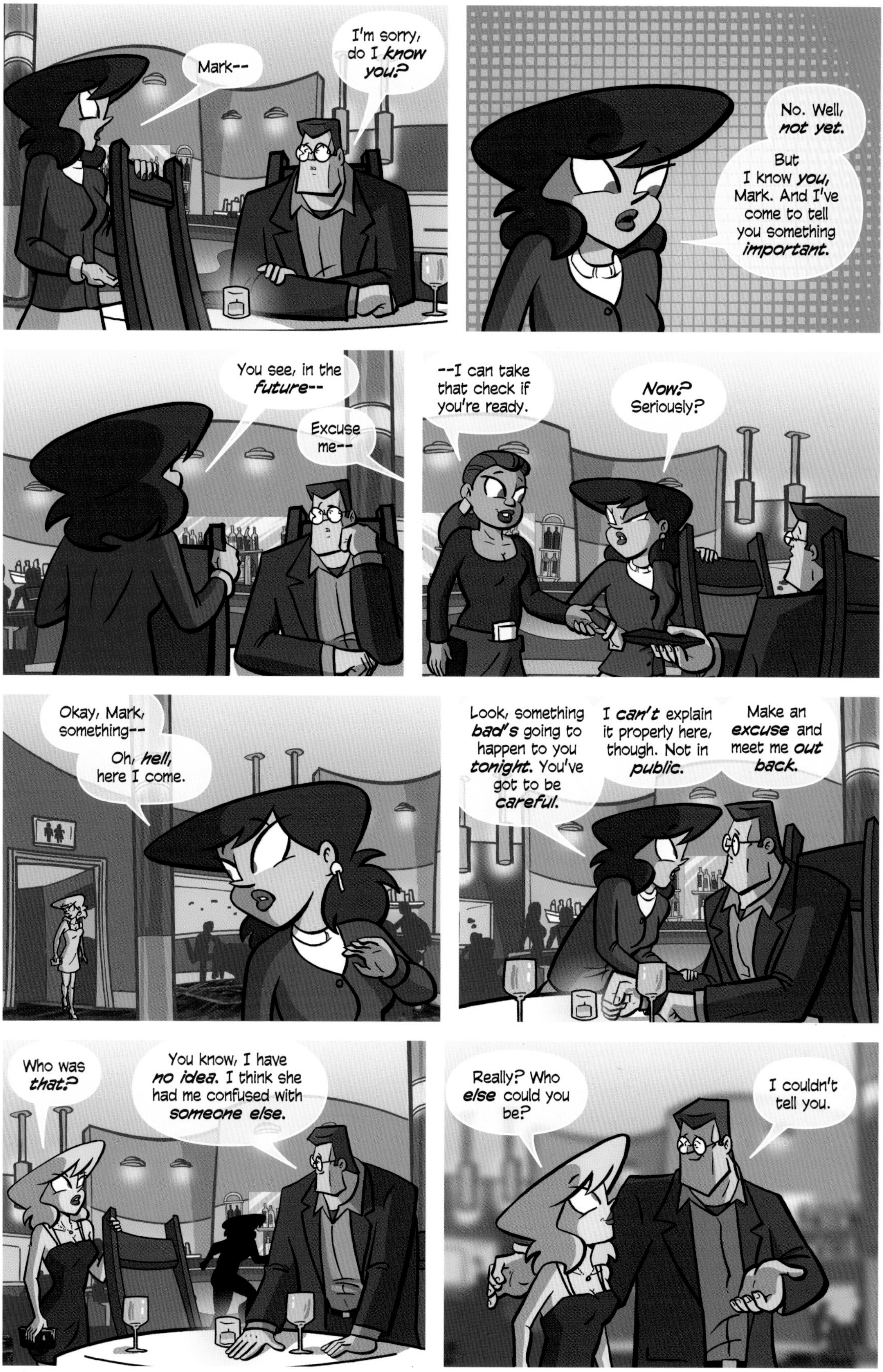
Mark--
I'm sorry, do I *know you?*
No. Well, *not yet.*
But I know *you,* Mark. And I've come to tell you something *important.*
You see, in the *future*--
Excuse me--
--I can take that check if you're ready.
Now? Seriously?
Okay, Mark, something--
Oh, *hell,* here I come.
Look, something *bad's* going to happen to you *tonight.* You've got to be *careful.*
I *can't* explain it properly here, though. Not in *public.*
Make an *excuse* and meet me *out back.*
Who was *that?*
You know, I have *no idea.* I think she had me confused with *someone else.*
Really? Who *else* could you be?
I couldn't tell you.

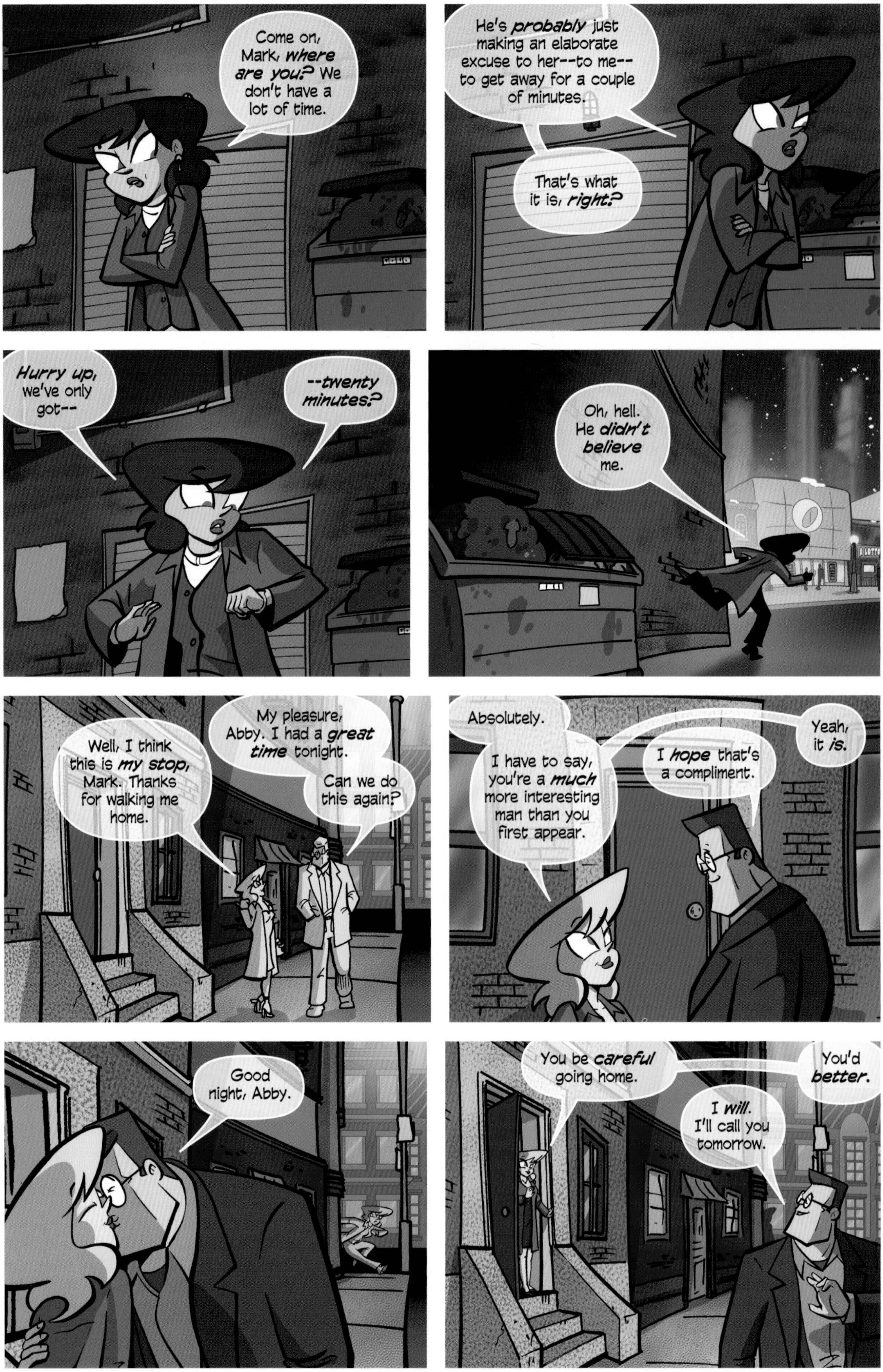
Come on, Mark, **where are you?** We don't have a lot of time.
He's **probably** just making an elaborate excuse to her--to me--to get away for a couple of minutes.
That's what it is, **right?**
Hurry up, we've only got--
--twenty minutes?
Oh, hell. He **didn't believe** me.
Well, I think this is **my stop,** Mark. Thanks for walking me home.
My pleasure, Abby. I had a **great time** tonight.
Can we do this again?
Absolutely.
I have to say, you're a **much** more interesting man than you first appear.
I **hope** that's a compliment.
Yeah, it **is.**
Good night, Abby.
You be **careful** going home.
I **will.** I'll call you tomorrow.
You'd **better.**

--no, Charlotte, it was great. I mean, *really* great.

It started off a *little* rocky, but then we just started clicking and never looked back.

"There's *more* to him than I thought."

Tonight? *Really*, North Korea?

Still, at least you waited until *after* my date.

He's *going*.

He's going to *die*.

"*I can't wait* to see *him* again."

Flawless? Well, no, I can't say that.

No, not him.

"This was all me."

I kind of blew the *dismount*.

¿Sigh! No, you dweeb, the *goodnight kiss*.

I just--I don't know, I think things were going *so* well that I got *worried* that things were going so well and I *tensed up*.

I didn't exactly deliver the *kiss that kills*.

Mark!

Wha--? Abby?

"But if I could do it over--

"...it'd be a *kiss to remember*."

Whoa.

That was--

-whoa.

Sorry.

No, don't be *sorry.*

I just had to say *goodbye* right. I've had...

...the time of my life.

Obviously.

Abby, I know we haven't known each other *long,* but I know you're *something special.* I'm looking forward to seeing *more* of you.

Um, but *right now,* I really have to *go.*

I know.

That's what I'm *afraid* of.

164

Wait, it's *midnight*. Mark was supposed to disappear at *11:58pm*. So--

--what? *Where* am I?

You are in the *city greens*, Abigail.

The Lady of the Flame has *returned you* to your home.

Home? But *Mark*-- what happened? *Why*--?

I have *good news* to share. You *succeeded* in restoring the timeline and saving Mark.

How did I-- hey, what time is it?

Ah, I also have *bad news*--

--'tis nearly *two* in the afternoon.

What?!

The *wedding's* at two!

Calm thyself, Abigail. I said 'tis *nearly* two.

We still have yet *fifteen* minutes. And, assuming no other catastophes, we can also avail ourselves the full resources of the *Liberty League*.

My compatriots have stayed disasters *countless* times. Your nuptials shall be *no more difficult*.

Now, let us away with *all due haste*. And tell me what you *require*.

First, a little *warning* next time.

Second, my *dress* and *Maid of Honor* to start.

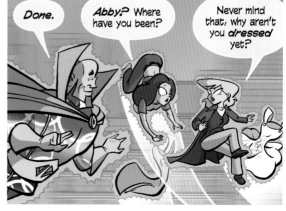

Done.

Abby? Where have you been?

Never mind that, why aren't you *dressed* yet?

Then...

--and *no one* can see us?

Nay. We are *invisible* to all. The screen is just for our benefit.

Geez, Mark is going to need super powers to get you *out* of this thing.

Okay, explain it again. *My kiss* saved Mark?

Aye. The Evil Brain's plan involved *split-second timing.* Your impromptu display of passion delayed the Crusader long enough to save him.

'Twas *truly* a kiss for the *ages.*

And to think that back in high school Billy McCormick said *I* was the better kisser.

Really? When's the last time one of *your* kisses changed the course of history?

And...

No, that's not--

--way too *I Dream of Jeannie*--

--whoa! That's it *exactly!*

Took you long enough.

Abby, I only became a licensed stylist *ninety seconds* ago!

Hey! I can see the church!

AT THE CHURCH...

--got it, Doc. We'll take care of everything on *our* end.

A *divergent timeline?* That's just bizarre.

Tell me about it.

All right, I need you to *distract Abby's brother* so I can get into the sacristy to talk to Mark.

Why do we need to distract Quincy?

Because my being here as your *"date"* explains why *Paul Lacroix* is at this wedding.

But it *wouldn't* explain why he went in to have a pre-wedding chat with a man he's *never met.*

Secret identities. *Feh.* More trouble than they're worth, I say.

Well, they *do* let you walk around unnoticed.

Although, in *your case,* that's probably impossible.

THE SACRISTY...

Paul, what are *you* doing here? Is *Abby* here yet? I can't hear her--

Abby's what I'm here to talk about. First, *don't panic,* everything's fine. But, um--

--the Evil Brain went *back in time* this morning and killed you three years ago.

Fortunately, Abby *wasn't* affected when the timeline realigned, and she was able to get our alternate counterparts to send her back in time to put things *back on track.*

Major Might and Windstar found his *lair,* but he was *already gone.*

Ha-ha-hah!

Oh, that's a *good one.*

Ah, Mark--?

You *are* joking, right?

Afraid not.

167

Oh God, oh God, I *can't* believe this. Is Abby all right?

Doc Karma says she's fine and *eager* to *get married*. Let's focus on *that*.

How? What if the *Celestial Hunger* attacks during the Mass? Or there's a *tsunami* while we're dancing our first dance? What if--?

Mark, *calm down*. The League's here for you, and I'm working on *something else* to keep things quiet, too.

Just worry about the *wedding*.

It wasn't *supposed* to be like this, you know. I just wanted a nice, *normal* wedding, now that ship has sailed.

Well, *maybe* I can get you the next best thing on that.

You were *supposed* to be my Best Man, and *that* couldn't happen--

How's *this?*

Mark, you *can* see me, right?

Zoe's mother lent me an *invisibility generator*.

Yeah, but only because I can see into the *ultraviolet spectrum*. What did you do?

I can't be your Best Man, but this way I can at least *stand with you*. Zoe's going to give Abby some contacts so she can see me, too.

Is this *all right?*

My best friend will be at my side when I get married. It's *more* than all right--

--it's *wonderful!*

What's wonderful, Marky Mark?

Um, ah, these *stretches*. Really loosen up the old back, Quincy.

MEANWHILE...

Doctor, everyone's in the church. The *coast is clear*.

As promised, Abigail, at the church with *three minutes* to spare.

Abby, a *moment*, please.

Amazonia, I'm in a bit of a *hurry* here.

I know, but Paul's turned himself *invisible* so he can stand *with* Mark--

--and he wanted you to have *these* so that *you* could see him, too.

Oh.

Okay.

Wow. You took that *right in stride.*

Well, it's not exactly the *weirdest* part of my day now, is it?

Abby! You're *here!*

Where have you *been?* We *tried* to call--

Yeah. There was a--

--*traffic* jam--

--*huge* accident.

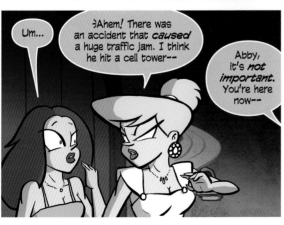

Um...

¿Ahem! There was an accident that *caused* a huge traffic jam. I think he hit a cell tower--

Abby, it's *not important.* You're here now--

--and we have a *walk* to *take.*

169

Whoa!

What is it, young Michael?

Abby's sister. I was so preoccupied with helping *Abby* that I didn't notice-- she is *hot!*

You're *also* now so preoccupied that you've forgotten--

"--exactly *how good* Mark's hearing is."

Whoops! *Sorry,* dude.

"Look at her, Paul. She's *absolutely stunning.*"

And in a few minutes, she's going to be *my* wife.

You're a *very* lucky man.

I am *indeed.*

So please tell me this isn't a *dream*--

--or a *hoax*--

--or an *imaginary story.*

Real as can *be,* buddy.

Mark, this is my *little girl*. You take good care of her.

I *will*, sir.

Hey.

Hey yourself.

I hear I *owe* you.

Yes, you *do*.

But, tell you what, *marry me*, and we'll call it *even*.

Deal.

And so...

Mark, Abigail, you have come *together* in this church so that the Lord may *seal* and *strengthen* your love.

Christ abundantly *blesses* this love. He has already consecrated you in baptism.

Now he enriches and strengthens you by a *special sacrament* so that you may assume the duties of marriage in mutual and lasting fidelity--

--in the presence of the Church's *minister* and this *community*, your *family* and *friends*.

Since it is your intention to enter into marriage, join hands--

--and *declare your consent* before God and his Church.

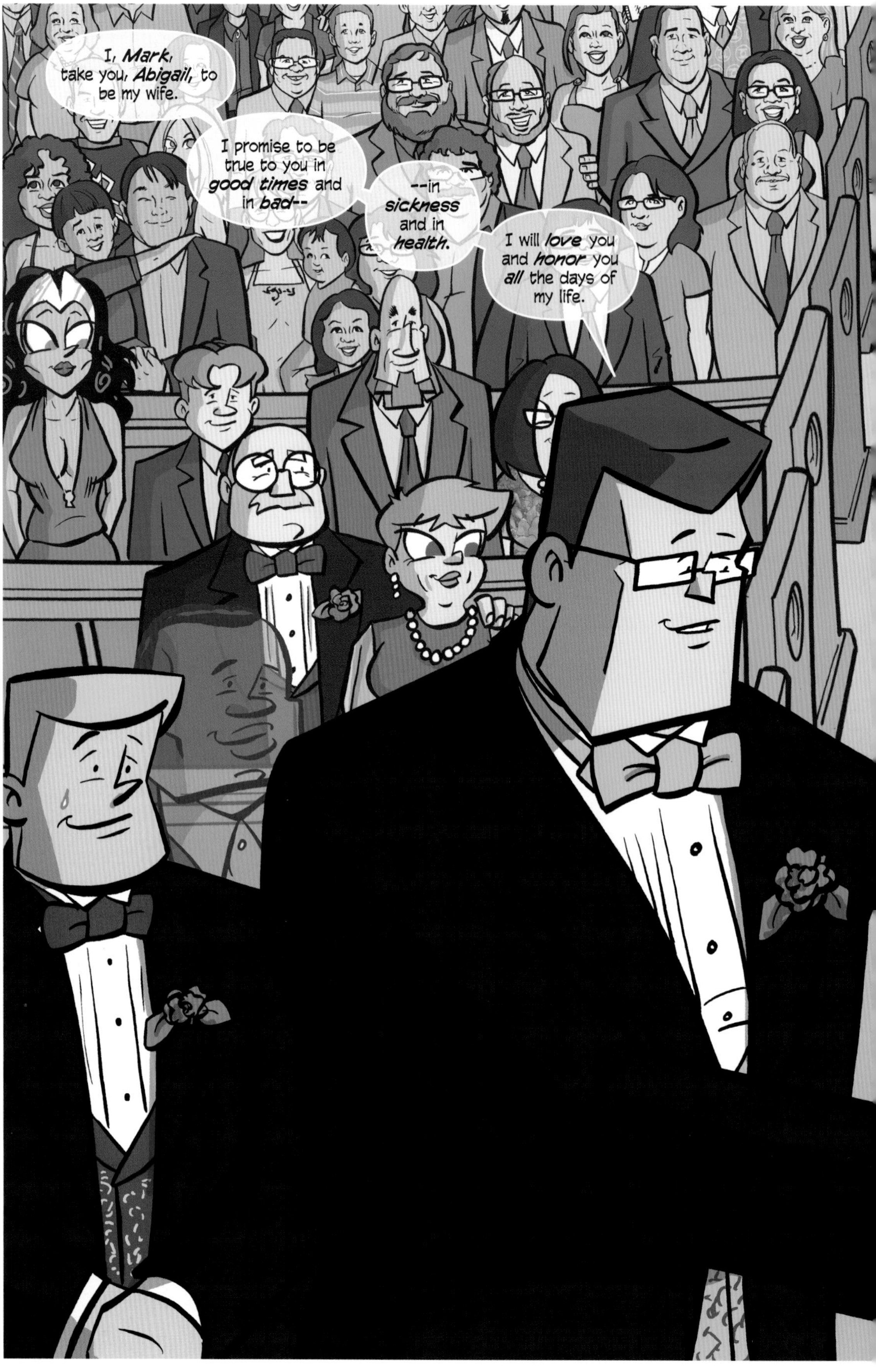
I, Mark, take you, Abigail, to be my wife.
I promise to be true to you in good times and in bad--
--in sickness and in health.
I will love you and honor you all the days of my life.

I now pronounce you *husband and wife.*

You may kiss the bride.

THEN... *CLAP! CLAP! CLAP! CLAP!*

You know, I have wanted to get you *alone* since you walked into that church.

The feeling is *more* than mutual--

YOU WENT BACK IN TIME?

--but obviously for *different* reasons.

SEVERAL EXPLANATIONS LATER...

--I *always wondered* why you came back to kiss me. Now I *know.*

I'm *sorry* you had to go through all that.

Don't be.

Right before I walked down that aisle, I got to see how *we* started. There's something *right* about that.

I'd certainly have *preferred* if your life hadn't been in jeopardy along the way, but, in its own way, it was a *gift.*

It really made me *appreciate* some things.

Did it, now? Like *what?*

Well, for *one* thing I'm very glad you don't have those *sideburns* anymore.

First, you've all made a *terrible mistake* giving the sportscaster the *mic*.

And, as you've probably guessed, I *am* going to talk about *sports*...and *Abby* and *Mark*.

When I was coming up as a sports reporter, I got to see, in person, *Omar Vizquel* and *Robbie Alomar* of the Cleveland Indians. These guys were, *hands down*, the *greatest* double play combination in the modern era.

The double play is turned all the time in baseball. But *these two*...seeing them work was *magic*. I watched them and said "One day, I'm going to tell my *grandkids* about this, that I had the honor to see the double play rise to level of *art*."

Tonight, all of *us* in this room have the *same privilege*.

Because, there have been *other* couples and *other* marriages, but tonight, with Abby and Mark-- you're seeing the one *you'll* tell *your* grandkids about.

To Abby and Mark!

Quincy, that was a *great* toast. But weren't you still in the *NFL* when Alomar got traded?

Yes, but the guy I hired to write my speech *wasn't*.

Whoa. That's a tough act to follow, but I'm going to try.

I always wanted my sister to find someone *special*. Someone sweet and funny and rich and good-looking--

--and most importantly, with a *richer* and *better* looking *younger* brother--

--and then she brought home *Mark*.

I mean, he was her *accountant*. How boring is *that?*

But then, a funny thing happened. I *got to know him*. And I found out there was a *special guy* behind those glasses--

--someone *as special* as *my sister*.

So join me in toasting Abby and Mark, and *their future*.

Our *future?* Sheesh! I'm just glad we got our *past* straightened out.

Me, too.

LATER...

So how are you *holding up?*

By my math, you've been up almost *thirty hours* now.

Oh, don't worry about *that.* On our way over here, Doc Karma cast an *anti-fatigue spell.*

I'm actually as *rested* as I've *ever* been.

Really? I'll have to thank him later--

--and I'll thank *you* later tonight.

THEN...

You did *really good* finding her, Mark.

Thanks, Mom, I'm partial to her myself.

You know, your father and I were always *worried* that you wouldn't find someone who'd appreciate how *super* you were.

Yeah, I'm sure my abilities make me pretty *high-maintenance.*

Oh, no, son--

--you were super *long before* you got your powers.

THEN...

All right, let's have all the *single ladies* on the dance floor for the bouquet toss.

Ready, everyone?

One--

--two--

--three!

That is just *totally unfair.*

AND...

And now it's time for the *garter toss.* Unattached gentlemen to the dance floor, please.

Whoops.

SPROING!

OW!

It's on the *ground!*

Mine!

No you don't!

Got it!

Deco City Defenders football *rules!*

I don't think I've been to a wedding where the boys were so *animated* about *catching the garter.*

You haven't been to a wedding where the winner got to put it on a *leggy, six-foot-tall princess warrior,* either.

177

Okay, we need *Quincy* out here now. It's time to put the garter on *Amazonia*.

Good luck, man!

Go for it!

And remember Quincy, every inch *above the knee* is *ten years' good luck* for the couple.

Hey.

Mark, with *those legs* you two ought to be good for a *couple hundred years*.

LATER...

Look at you, all those *curves,* and me with *no brakes.*

Um, do I *know you?*

We *flew in* together... with the *doctor.*

Oh, sorry, I *didn't recognize* you without the--

You're the *speedster guy,* right?

Yeah, that's why we *wear* them.

Blurstreak.

Fastest man on the planet.

Yeah, you *realize* that's not really a *selling point,* right?

ELSEWHERE...

--yeah, his tie changes *eleven times* in that scene.

Really? I've seen that movie three times and *never* noticed it.

Sorry, I'm probably *boring* you. You just got me talking about movies and I got all *wound up.*

Not *at all.* You're studying film, you *should* be passionate about it.

In fact, maybe sometime *we* should--

Here's your drink, Jason. Hey, *who's this?*

Oh, *please*, like you don't know *Amazonia. Amazonia*, this is my *boyfriend*, Eric.

Now you were *saying* something?

What? Oh, nothing important.

So, how long have you two known each other?

LATER...

Well, I just almost tried to pick up a gay guy. How's *your* night going?

Blurstreak came over and--

Say no more. Sounds like we're having the same kind of luck.

It'd be easier to take if my sister hadn't *skimped* on the liquor. She could have gone *top shelf.*

Here you go. It's *ambrosia.*

You brought a *flask* to the wedding?

To my *ex-boyfriend's wedding?* Yeah.

See, that's what I like about you *hero types.* You're *always* prepared.

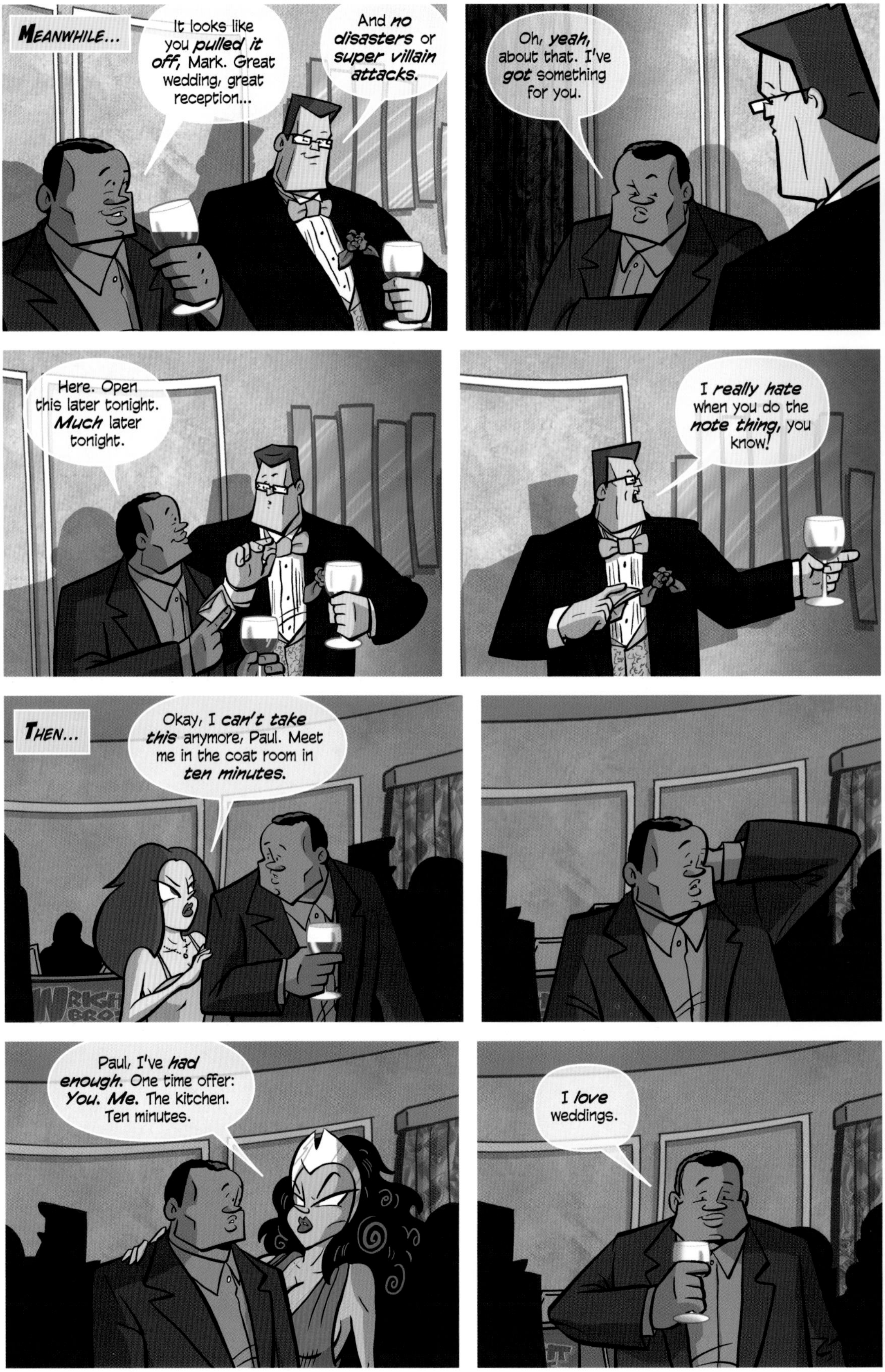
Meanwhile...
It looks like you pulled it off, Mark. Great wedding, great reception...
And no disasters or super villain attacks.
Oh, yeah, about that. I've got something for you.
Here. Open this later tonight. Much later tonight.
I really hate when you do the note thing, you know!
Then...
Okay, I can't take this anymore, Paul. Meet me in the coat room in ten minutes.
Paul, I've had enough. One time offer: You. Me. The kitchen. Ten minutes.
I love weddings.

FINALLY...

Mom, Dad, I think we're going to be *leaving*.

Thank you *so much* for everything.

Our *pleasure*, dear.

Why did Abby's aunt have to be a *travel agent?*

People fly *in* planes all the time, son. It'll be fine.

Enjoy the ride-- and *Hawaii*.

We'll call you when we get back--

--Mom.

You know, I don't know that I've ever seen my Mom *speechless* before.

Then it's *true* what they say: today *is* the happiest day of my life.

I think that's *everyone*, Mrs. Spencer. Are you ready?

I am *indeed* Mr. Spencer. Let's g--

SPENCER TENNYSON WEDDING RECEPTION

--oh!

ZOOM

BOOOM!

Was that *thunder?*

Sonic boom.

What?

Huh? *Sorry.* I meant thunder.

EARLY THE NEXT MORNING...

WHUMP!

Gah! Stupid--

Unnh... Mark, is that you?

Yeah, *sorry.* I was *trying* to be quiet. Guess I'm going to have to work on that.

Where are *you* off to?

Well...

Yesterday.

You're going back in time? *Why?*

You know how--aside from your side trip--there were no disasters or robberies or *anything?*

Paul said he could figure out a way to keep yesterday *quiet* so *all* my friends and I could have an uninterrupted day.

He did. His idea is to use the Evil Brain's time machine to send me back *twenty-four hours.* Then *I* can patrol while the past me has his perfect wedding.

And you were sneaking out without telling me because you just wanted it to be a *secret gift,* right?

Yeah, pretty much.

Then don't worry about it. I'm *glad* you woke me.

Because I want to *come with you.*

What?

182

Mark, I've still got Doc Karma's *illusion bracelet*. I could go back and see my *own wedding!*

There's *so much* that happened, it's all a bit of a *blur*. I'd love to get the chance to *see it again.*

Well, it's not like *I* wasn't going to *peek* in myself.

C'mon, get *dressed.*

Now, you'll have to be careful not to do anything to *change the future.*

This isn't my *first* time travel trip, you know.

Besides, I think my future's *perfect* just the way it is.

END

183

So, I was trying to think of some way to make the *Love and Capes* wedding a Big Thing, as well as to maybe generate some revenue and press. I started thinking about doing a print, and I thought about the famous image of the wedding of Reed and Sue of the Fantastic Four. I considered an homage image, but realized that I didn't have enough pre-existing characters to fill the church. Where would I get them?

That's when I realized I could open it up to my readers. I started my professional art career as a caricaturist, and still do a fair amount of work as one. I could do caricatures of *Love and Capes* fans at the wedding. So I made the offer available online.

It went better than I could have possibly imagined.

I always try to be prepared, so I had a plan to do two covers, but I never thought I'd need to. I was humbled by the response. I really have the best fans on the planet.

A. QUINCY TENNYSON
B. DARKBLADE/PAUL LACROIX
C. AMAZONIA
D. JEROME SPENCER
E. JOANNE SPENCER
F. CHARLOTTE TENNYSON
G. CATHERINE TENNYSON
H. MILES TENNYSON

1. SHANA SOMMERMAN
   ED SOMMERMAN
   HAYDEN SOMMERMAN
   ALEXIS SOMMERMAN
2. BOB BRETALL
3. PAB SUNGENIS
   BRYAN IRRERA
4. BEN DiFEO
   JENI DiFEO
5. LOUIE LA PALOMBARA III
   DEBI LIPPENCOTT
6. BLAKE PETIT
   ERIN BLASH
7. JESSE JACKSON
   LINDA JACKSON
8. ANGELA PAMAN
9. MARK GEIER
10. MARK BOSS
    KAREN FENECH
11. VINCENT KREJCI
12. ALEX JOHNSON
    KATHY JOHNSON
13. DAVID BEAVEN JR.
    ANDREA GRABOW
    ALLEN WILKINSON
14. IAN LEVENSTEIN
15. THE DEFUSER
    NORMA CRIPPEN
16. FEEDBACK
    MRS. FEEDBACK
17. SPAZDOG

18. JOEL SCHULDT
19. MIKE ZAHLER
    NORMAN ZAHLER
    THOM ZAHLER
    JOHN ZAHLER
    ROBERT ZAHLER
    DAVID ZAHLER
    AMBER ZAHLER
    KAYLEE ZAHLER (FRONT)
20. MARC BOWKER
    ANGIE BOWKER
21. DOMINIK SON
    EUGENE SON
    NICOLE SON
    BRIGITTA SON
    KATERI SON
22. DWAYNE McDUFFIE
    CHARLOTTE FULLERTON
23. DAVID PHELPS
    MELISSA PHELPS
24. MATTHEW BARNETT
    TIMOTHY BARNETT
25. MARK POULTON
    CHRISSY POULTON
26. BRIAN COX
    KATY COX
27. ALBERT HOOD
28. CATT WILLIAMS
    CHRIS BURNAM
29. JOHNATHAN ALEXANDER WOO
    SHARYN LESLEY MAH
    BRANDON ALEXANDER MAH
    SAMANTHA LESLIE MAH
    GARY POON MAH
    JAMES DOUGLAS MAH
    ASHLEY MARIE WOO
    CHRISTOPHER ALLEN WOO
    DENISE MARIE WOO
    MAY HUANG WOO
    KEVIN WESLEY WOO
    KONNER DANIEL WOO
    KAMERON JUSTIN WOO
    JOHN YUM WOO
    MAY QUAN WOO

30. CHRIS PENNEY
31. JORDAN FARRELL
32. RON CURELL
PAM CURELL
33. BARB KUSZNIR
ROMAN KUSZNIR
34. JUNE LEE
35. KARA FRYE
DAN FRYE
36. ANTHONY WILLIAMS
CHEROKEE WILLIAMS
37. WESLEY JOHNSON
38. BRYCE WEBER
CRAIG WEBER
CONNOR WEBER
39. CHRISTOPHER STRICKLAND
40. SUMMER BLANK
ALAN BLANK
SONG BLANK
41. JUNIOR BLANCO
JENNIFER BLANCO
42. MICHAEL BOATMAN
43. ADRIANA PEREZ
JOE FORNADEL
44. SHAWN "KWIP" WILLIAMS
JAMIE "DR. SEXY" FICKES
JASON "HAPPYJACK" MEADOWS
"MAD" RUSTY MECK
45. CHRISTOPHER BENITEZ
46. FIONA GLENNANNE
SANDI SCHEIDERER
47. GLENN HAKANSON
HELEN HAKANSON
48. JEANETTA ADKINS
ANDREW NIXON
49. AMY YOUNG
50. HOYT SPENCER
MEGHAN BRENNAN

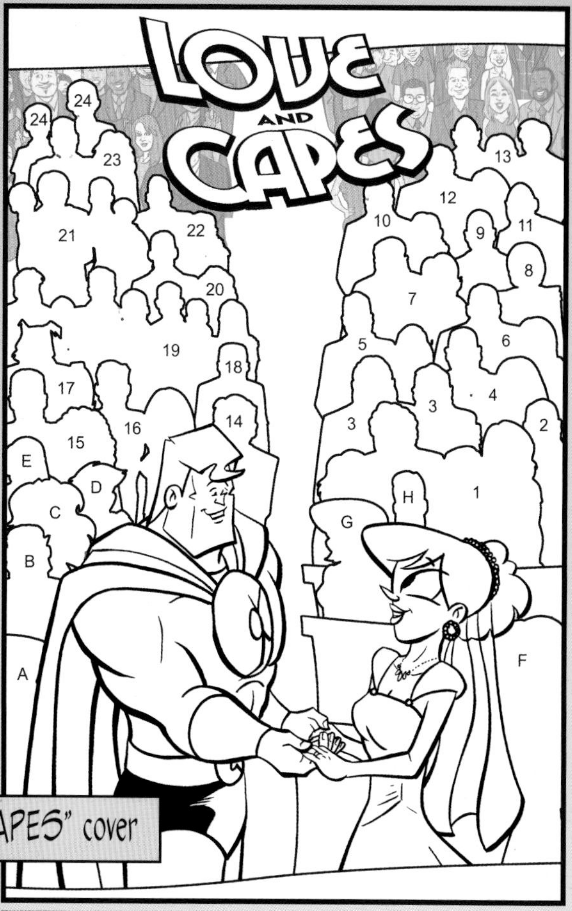
LOVE AND CAPES

"CAPES" cover

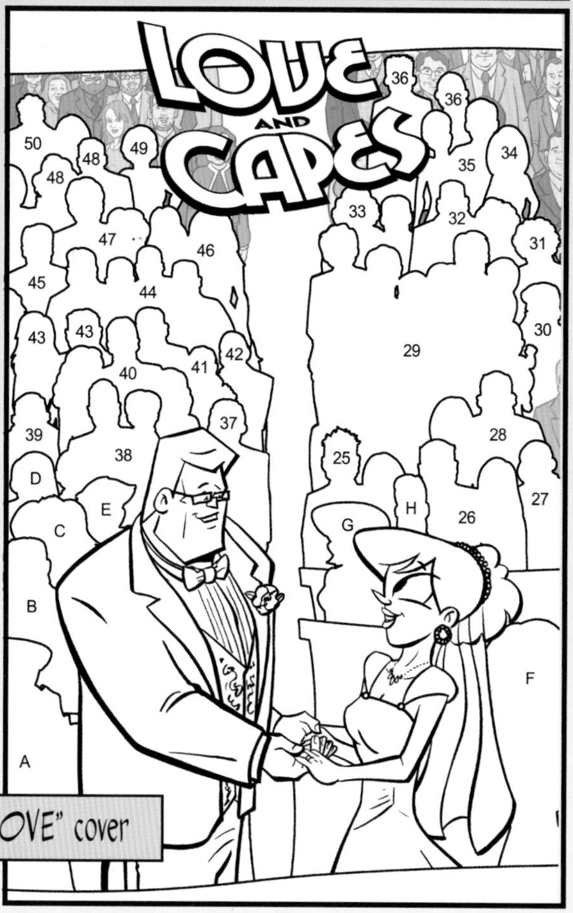
LOVE AND CAPES

"LOVE" cover

BEHIND THE SCENES

I ALWAYS KNEW ISSUE #6 WOULD END WITH THE COAL-INTO-DIAMONDS SCENE, but that was as far as I went. I never considered how Mark would actually ask Abby to marry him when I got to issue #7.

The only thing I had in my mind was that much-maligned moment in *Notting Hill* where Julia Roberts says "I'm just a girl, standing in front of a boy, asking him to love her." I thought it'd be cool to do a moment where Mark, without his glasses/disguise and not as the Crusader, is the one who asks the question.

If I had planned this scene out with that clarity back when I did issue one, we never would have seen Mark without his glasses when out of uniform. Oh, well, hindsight's always 20/20.

Also, the character of Steel Worker (seen on the cover) was created to give a bit of a tie-in to the *Iron Man* movie, since both this issue and the movie came out on Free Comic Book Day. On the retail version, to differentiate them, I replaced Steel Worker with Major Might.

I STARTED FEELING COCKY WITH ISSUE #8. I decided to do a continued issue, which is always a dicey proposition for a quarterly comic. When people asked what the new issue was going to be about, I referenced Marvel's *Secret Invasion* series featuring the shape-shifting Skrulls. "Mark's a Skrull" I would say. They'd laugh, not realizing that I was actually going to do that story.

I also felt bad that Darkblade had never been on a cover at that point, and tried to come up with a design featuring him. Finally, I decided to go for broke and just have him yelling at me about his lack of cover time. (And, for those of you who think that I draw myself as the Crusader, this showed how I'd actually draw myself.)

Part of this issue was inspired by doing an interview for Sequential Tart. My interviewer asked me if we'd ever see the Crusader on Ice special mentioned in issue #3. I hadn't planned on it, but when I was asked the question, the idea hit me fully formed: a bootleg at a comic convention!

Then I started to write the lyrics for the Crusader song when I realized I didn't need to. You see, I send every issue, page by page, to my "Secret Society of Super Reviewers," a group of trusted friends and colleagues who backstop me on plot and spelling.

Among them is my friend Mike Bokausek. I knew when he saw my attempt at a Crusader song, he'd just write a better one and e-mail it to me. So, no fool I, I asked him to write the song outright. He did, and presented in its entirety on the next page is the full text of the *Crusader on Ice* song…

THE CRUSADER ON ICE
lyrics by Mike Bokausek

A large group of skaters, dressed in various business suits and carrying briefcases, comes out of the entry tunnel (disguised not so subtlely as a subway entrance) and onto the ice. The various men and women skate around in random fashion for a time until, at center ice, a male skater and female skater pass by each other. As they pass, they point to each other then circle back, where they link for a twirl before stopping to talk. They are BILL and JANE.

Bill: Say Jane!

Jane: Hey Bill!

Bill: How've ya' been?

Jane: Great! Hey did you just get into town?

Bill: Yes I did. I just got transferred here to big 'ol Deco City.

Jane: So how do you like it so far?

Bill: Like it? I love it! It's so much bigger and more exciting than back home!

Jane: So have you—

[They are interrupted by a loud alarm sounding nearby. All the skaters freeze as the overhead lights flash red and six new skaters shoot out of the entry tunnel. The new skaters are all wearing masks, carrying prop guns and holding sacks with large "$" symbols on the side. They skate in a line through the frozen skaters, occasionally pushing them over, and, finally, they skate between our original couple.]

Bill: My gosh, Jane! I think they just robbed the Deco City National Bank! Shouldn't someone call the police?

Jane: Hah hah! You really are new in town!

[As she finishes, the lights turn off and a loud drumroll/rhythmic pounding begins. The lights begin to strobe and we see (partially) a red and yellow figure come out of the entry tunnel, skating quickly and efficiently between the frozen skaters, now including the "frozen" thieves. As the red-and-yellow figure reaches the front of the line of thieves, he stops, the drumming stops and the normal lights come on.

We now clearly see the CRUSADER standing in front of the thieves with his arms folded.]

Crusader: Isn't it a little early to be making such a big withdrawal?

Lead thief: It's the Crusader, boys! Get 'im!

[As the six thieves encircle the calmly standing Crusader, the other skaters form up into a chorus, fronted by Bill and Jane. As the Crusader begins to fight with the thieves, Bill, Jane and the chorus begin to sing:]

Whenever crime's afoot in Deco City's streets

it seems there's just one person that those criminals will meet

no matter what the time, to us it always seems

there's just one strapping hero who will answer the screams

When villains come a calling, whether Blob or Evil Brain

we always know the score and it follows a refrain

He flies onto the scene, showing bad guys there's none greater

He's Deco City's defender and we call him THE CRUSADER!

He soars! He fights!

He dresses up in tights!

He rights. The wrongs!

He's really super strong!

Our red and golden warrior in underwear that's long!

He's the Crusader -- in flight!

[By this time, Crusader has finished off three of the bad guys. The remaining three begin picking up various props with which to begin bashing the Crusader while the chorus sings the next few verses.]

He saves the world from meteors and sends villains to their knees

but takes the time from fighting crime to save kittens stuck in trees

He's always there to save us. He's the one who calms our fears

He's the reason that no plane's crashed here for nearly seven years

He soars among the clouds, wind whipping through his hair

looking down upon us, evil shrinking from his stare

For justice, truth and honor are his modus operandi

He's never dark or broody when apprehending bad guys

He's like. A boy scout.

Bad words he'll never shout.

His costume. Has bulges.

and he never quite divulges

just who he really is, so you will have to indulge us!

He's the Crusader -- in flight!

[The music continues as we see only one thief left. He takes off and the Crusader pursues. The thief and the Crusader pass between Bill and Jane.]

Bill: Wow! He really is amazing!

Jane: I'll say.

Bill: Say, do you think he could lift up a car?

Jane: Of course.

Bill: Do you think he could pick up a house?

Jane: No problem.

Bill: Could he pick up the Deco City Building?

Jane: Hmmm. . . I don't know about that, but he could pick ME up anytime!

Bill: Me too!

Jane: What?

Bill: Nothing.

[The chorus cheers as we see that the Crusader has finally caught up to the last thief, who is cornered in an alleyway set and pulls out a gun.]

Thief: I'm warning you Crusader. Back off or else!

Crusader: Or else what?

Thief: All right. I warned you.

[The thief shoots and sparks fly off of the Crusader's chest.]

Crusader: Wow. You must REALLY be new in town.

[Crusader then punches the last thief, who goes flying through the "wall" of the alley, leaving a large hole. The sound of tweeting birds is heard. The CHORUS cheers as the music rises:]

He soars! He fights!

He dresses up in tights!

He rights. The wrongs!

He's really super strong!

Our red and golden warrior in underwear that's long!

He's the Crusader -- in flight!

PART OF THE GOAL WITH ISSUE #8 WAS TO REDEEM AMAZONIA after her tell-all book stunt from issue #6. She had to do her season of penance. Issue #9 allowed me to mess

her right back up, thanks to Psi-Clone stealing Mark's identity.

Psi-Clone himself featured a costume design from a character I created as a kid. Back then, he was called Infil Traitor, and was designed for the Masters of the Universe 1986 "Create a Figure" contest.

Sadly, I didn't win. But no idea ever goes to waste.

I thought Psi-Clone using his borrowed memories to take advantage of Amazonia was a perfect way to reset the character to her issue #1 pining lover state.

It would also set up Amazonia's closer relationship with Darkblade, which even took **me** by surprise.

AND NOW WE COME TO THE FIRST ISSUE I WAS EVER SCARED TO WRITE.

Deciding to give Abby super powers, admittedly not an original idea for a superhero story, was easy, but I had to think of a good way for her to then lose those powers. I thought about giving her a 24-hour time limit, but there was too much hero stuff I wanted to cover to fit it in.

ORIGINALLY, THE RETAIL COVER WAS GOING TO FEATURE AN ALTERNATE COLOR SCHEME FOR ABBY'S COSTUME. BUT I HAD SUCH TROUBLE FIGURING OUT ONE COLOR TREATMENT THAT I LIKED I COULDN'T DO A SECOND. SO, ALL THAT CHANGED WERE THE COLOR BARS AND BACKGROUND.

Then it hit me: What if they were permanent… until Abby decided to give them up.

There was my conflict. Abby's a good person. If she got super powers, she'd want to keep them to serve humanity. Unless, of course, something so terrible happened to her that she didn't want to have them anymore.

I'd frequently used the line "First rule of wearing a cape: You can't save everyone." I decided that issue #10 was going to illustrate that.

So I found myself writing, for lack of a better comparison, a "very special episode" of *Love and Capes*. It was like that episode of *Family Ties* where Alex's friend dies and he spends the whole show in an open stage set in his psychiatrist's office. It was the issue with a different tone and bittersweet ending.

I had a mantra while writing this issue: I had to stick the landing. If I was going to write the first real downer ending of the series, it'd have to be one of the best things I'd ever written. It was fairly daunting, but I'm pretty happy with the result.

I'm always impressed by doctors, police, firefighters and the like. If I make a mistake at my job, no one dies. Not so with them. That's Abby's story in this issue. Deep down, she doesn't want to have Mark's job. I believe that if Abby were granted super powers irrevocably, she would have found a way to deal with the burden, but she'd prefer not to be put to the test.

Seriousness aside, there's a lot of funny in this story, too. I love the costume trying scene. A lot of female comic characters have pretty impractical outfits, including Amazonia, so it was nice to make fun of that.

Here's a little "Where do you get your ideas from" for you, too. I was at a convention talking with a cosplayer. She mentioned she liked both Batgirl and Wonder Woman. "So, who would you dress as if you could?" I asked.

"Batgirl. The cape covers your rear."

I opened up the notepad on my iPhone and wrote that down right away.

When the issue came out, all my work paid off. *Love and Capes #10* is probably the best reviewed issue of the series.

In issue #11, Amazonia's storyline took another turn. I knew she had to be at the wedding, and that Abby wouldn't invite her, if left to her own designs. And so began the Quest for the Dress storyline.

Add to that the idea of Abby and Amazonia getting drunk together and having a bonding moment was too good to pass up. It also let me flesh out (pun intended) much more of Amazonia's character.

We also got to see her homeworld. The general look of Leandia is inspired by the 1980 *Flash Gordon* movie. Yeah, I know it's not a great film, but man is it fun. From it I got the bright colors, the skimpy costumes and the exotic locales that became Zoe's homeworld.

I left some things on the table there, too. There was a whole explanation about how only members of the royal family have super powers, and reasoning why those floating discs were actually safe to use. But, fun as that stuff was, it wasn't as important as the main story, and so it was cut.

With issue #12, we hit the second story I was really worried about writing. If you spend eleven issues building up to something, it better be something special.

In interviews I made a lot of references to the wedding episode of *Lois and Clark*, which featured Delta Burke as "The Wedding Destroyer." I promised it would be nothing like that. I liked the series, but that episode was a bit of a low point.

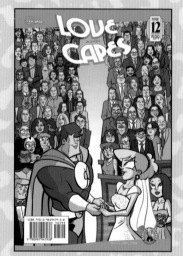

I'd been setting up this story since #10. Remember how Doc Karma says he can't read Abby on page two? That wasn't just a joke, but me laying the foundation. I had also wanted to reference a recurring argument between Mark and Abby where he insisted she kissed him twice on their first date. Abby would steadfastly say she'd only kissed him once because she hadn't kissed him the second time... yet.

Unfortunately, it took too much to reference that in any previous issue. And, I couldn't make the time travel causality work right. If Mark remembered both kisses, then they were living in the "correct" reality, so why would Abby suddenly wake up in the wrong one? And, a plotline involving Future Abby spilling a potion on Past Abby to make her immune to the changes in the timeline made less sense. So I relied on the Lady of the Flame to help things glide along. Not what I'd planned, but still a nifty solution.

The idea that we'd go back in time to Mark and Abby's first date was inspired by my friend Jesse Jackson (no, not that one) who really wanted to see that first date. I'm glad I listened to him. It was a really interesting time to explore.

Heck, when I was writing it I wound up learning about my own characters. When I wrote that first date, I realized that Mark and Abby shouldn't have worked on that first date. Mark would spend the whole date lying to her, because he'd have to. Then

I had the epiphany that they were both readers, and that was their initial common bond. With that, everything clicked.

The Evil Brain was an issue, too. I knew after three years of referencing him, he should be the big bad in this issue, but I liked that he was never seen in the book, kind of like Norm's wife on *Cheers*. Having him steal people's bodies allowed him to make his first appearance without ever really appearing.

I also decided that while anything before the wedding was fair game for disaster, the wedding itself had to be a straight-up wedding. My characters deserved it. So notice that once Abby enters the church, everything goes smoothly.

I have to say, I was emotionally spent after finishing this one. Writing the perfect ending took a lot out of me, and I was ready for a break. I didn't get one, as I had to start #13 almost the next day.

But that's a story for another time.

THE ISSUE THAT ALMOST WAS

AS I WAS FINISHING UP #11, I FOUND OUT THAT I WAS NOMINATED FOR A HARVEY AWARD FOR BEST CARTOONIST FOR LOVE AND CAPES. I'd eventually lose to Al Jaffee, and there's no shame in that. Marc Nathan, owner of the excellent Baltimore Comicon and sponsor of the Harveys, suggested that I do a special con issue of the book. Maybe a kind of "clip show."

The idea was too good for me to let go. I had plans to make issue #11½ the bachelor party, since that didn't fit in #11 or #12. With *Love and Capes*' sitcom roots, doing a recap show seemed perfect. I had the idea that while Mark and Quincy were at his bachelor party, Amazonia and the other super heroines would take Abby out for a bachelorette party. It'd be my way to have characters ask, "So, Abby, how did Mark tell you he was the Crusader?" and cue the harps to fade to a flashback. Plus, I could have dropped my "two kisses" idea into that story.

THE BALTIMORE VERSION OF 11½

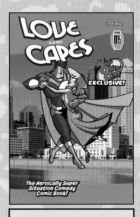

THE MID-OHIO-CON VERSION OF 11½

Unfortunately, my eyes were bigger than my stomach. Or my drawing hand. Or something like that. I just couldn't do the clip show book and get #12 done on time. But, while I was working on #12, I realized the first twelve pages were an absolutely perfect preview. Page 12 even ended with a perfect cliffhanger. All I had to add was a cover or two for both Mid-Ohio-Con and Baltimore, where the book would be released.

So, if you missed those issues, don't worry, you didn't miss anything but these two covers, reproduced here, and two darn fine conventions.

LOVE AND CAPES

WRITTEN AND DRAWN BY THOMAS F. ZAHLER

Thom Zahler was an aspiring cartoonist test piloting a new experimental drafting chair when an adjustment went out of control. The chair crashed and Zahler was left a man barely alive.

Joe Kubert of the Joe Kubert School looked at the wreckage of a man and said, "Gentlemen, we can rebuild him. We have the technology. We have the capability to make the world's first bionic cartoonist. We can make him better than he was before. Better. Funnier. Cartoonier."

Donning a red track suit, Thom Zahler became the Six Million Dollar Cartoonist.*

Since then, he's cartooned for cartoonitoriums all across the world. He's worked for the Cleveland Indians, the Colorado Rockies, Learn-It Systems, Claypool Comics, Lone Star Press, IDW Publishing, Prilosec, and many others. In 2009, he was nominated for a Harvey Award for Best Cartoonist. He lost to Al Jaffee, of *Mad Magazine* fame.

Thom suspects that Mr. Jaffee may also be a cyborg.

* Six million dollars being the Kubert School tuition, adjusted for inflation and maximum comedy.

SPECIAL THANKS TO:
AMY WOLFRAM, BILL WILLIAMS,
DEITRI VILLARREAL,
PAUL D. STORRIE, SANDI SCHEIDERER,
JILL A. SMITH, ROGER PRICE,
PAUL MEROLLE, CHRISTINE MARGALIS,
JESSE JACKSON, MIKE HORKAN,
MATT HALEY,
CHARLOTTE FULLERTON,
CARIDAD FERRER,
HARLAN & SUSAN ELLISON,
AND MIKE BOKAUSEK